THROWN AWAY CHILDREN

Stella's
Story

THROWN AWAY **CHILDREN**

Stella's Story

Louise Allen

with Theresa McEvoy

MIRROR BOOKS

First published by Mirror Books in 2020

Mirror Books is part of Reach plc
10 Lower Thames Street
London EC3R 6EN

www.mirrorbooks.co.uk

ISBN 978-1-912624-88-1

Typeset by Danny Lyle

Printed and bound in Great Britain by
CPI Group (UK) Ltd, Croydon, CR0 4YY

A CIP catalogue record for this book is available from the British Library.

Every effort has been made to fulfil requirements with regard to
reproducing copyright material. The author and publisher will be
glad to rectify any omissions at the earliest opportunity.

3 5 7 9 10 8 6 4

Cover image: iStock
(Posed by model)

To all the children and adults who have
experienced abuse, neglect and the care system,
I write my books and speak loudly for you

To those of you who have the power and influence to
help people like me and improve the broken system,
I beg you to speak up

Contents

Part One

I

OCTOBER

Its happening RITE NOW pls come

Shannon hits 'send' on her mobile phone just in time before the next wave of pain engulfs her whole body. She screws up her eyes so that they are shut tight, not knowing quite why that helps. When the pain recedes almost as quickly as it came and she is able to open her eyes again, she is dazzled by the brightness of the room once more. Above her, clinical white walls dissect white tiles at sharp right angles, illuminated by a fluorescent strip bulb. She feels suffocated by the bleaching whiteness. It is all so hopelessly unforgiving inside here. The windows gape black against all the white and light of the room. It seems to have got so dark outside so fast. Or has she been here much longer than she thinks?

Shannon is vaguely aware of some music playing in the background. The track sounds familiar, though she can't quite register the song itself, or even make out any lyrics.

3

The playlist that she made for giving birth doesn't really seem to be helping. She had planned for the final track to be Underworld's *Born Slippy* – old now, but classic – though it feels as though that moment is a long, long way off yet. She needs more than music to help her now. Isn't there meant to be some sort of pain relief?

Where is he? She thinks. *I need him here! I hate him. Where the hell is he? Terry. Terry. Don't do this. Where are you?*

Shannon oscillates between wanting Terry right there with her by her side – and despising him for getting her into this state. How is it fair that he can just up and go, leaving her to do this bit all by herself? One minute she wishes he was there holding her hand, massaging her aching back, stroking her forehead; the next she knows she wants to do this all on her own. It is her moment.

Even the midwife had seemed surprised when Shannon arrived at the hospital alone. 'No one at all? Not a partner? Your mum? A friend? There must be *someone* I can call for you, love?'

Shannon had thought about calling the girls, Vivi and Tara. They had joked about being 'birth partners' for her when she was much earlier in the pregnancy. But Shannon doesn't really think that they would be a great deal of help, and she doesn't want to give any satisfaction to this midwife, who is a condescending bitch anyway. Who is she to call Shannon 'love'? Shannon can still hear the judgement ringing in the midwife's voice when she was admitted to the labour ward an hour or so earlier.

'You're just a child yourself. Are you sure I can't get your mum here?' Not just judgemental but downright unsupportive. 'It's not usual to do this on your own, you know.' What was 'usual' anyway? And a midwife shouldn't be passing comment on her choices anyway. She can do what she likes. This woman is exactly the opposite of what a midwife is supposed to be, Shannon is sure. She remembers reading that the healthcare professionals are supposed to respect your decisions. Right now she doesn't feel as though any of her decisions have been respected, inside the hospital or out of it.

But with each contraction bringing her closer to the most important thing she has ever done, Shannon hurts so, so badly. And the stupid midwife is right: she doesn't really want to be all on her own. She shouldn't be all alone. He promised. He promised.

But he has broken promises before.

And things are tricky for Terry right now, she reminds herself. He's trying to lie low after a little deal that went wrong last week. It wasn't his fault. Shannon knows that he can't risk being where the police might be able to find him easily. But she still can't entirely shake away the nagging doubts that the baby has been keeping him away, too. She has tried to stay 'fun' all the way through the pregnancy, but hormones have made her tired and grumpy at times, however much she has tried to ignore them. And it's difficult to feel attractive when you are lugging around a belly as large as this one. It's bigger than a ripe watermelon. Though

Shannon has worked hard to keep herself looking good – not like some, who let themselves go once they start to show. She has positively glowed inside each time someone has told her what a neat bump she has, friends and strangers alike.

Perhaps she should have told her mother about the baby, after all. Even after everything that happened between them. It's not like Shannon hasn't thought about it over the last few months. But how hard had her parents tried to find her when she left? Really? Shannon didn't even get a birthday card last week. But then, be fair, she thinks. She hasn't told her mother where she is living these days. Her mother wouldn't approve of the flat, nor the neighbourhood, and definitely not Terry.

The birthday was her 17th, and now she is experiencing another 'birthday' – but this one doesn't feel anything like a celebration. Shannon actually feels like giving up now. That's it, she decides. She isn't going to do it. She wants out. She wants out of this whole deal: pregnancy, baby, the lot. She is too young for any of this. It wasn't meant to be. She wants it all to stop. She didn't sign up for this. Not the pain, not the being alone, not the bloody baby. None of it. She wants out. But the baby inside her doesn't, yet.

Terry, the sod, is still not replying to her message. Fathers are supposed to be there at the birth of their children these days, aren't they? Assuming, of course, that Terry *is* the father. But, in practical terms, Terry is the best bet she has, currently.

Where are you?

Her fingers press 'send' again while her brain tells her that the messages are making her sound desperate. Right now, though, Shannon *is* desperate. Though it probably isn't the best plan to let Terry know how desperate. He can be quite manipulative when he wants to be. She tells herself that millions of women have done this before her – given birth. She is not the first teenager to do this. She is young and fit and tough. She braces for the next contraction. Now the midwife is by her side and stroking her back and telling her how well she is doing, how brave she is being, as Shannon screams out, colouring the white walls blue with creative obscenities.

'That's some choice language you've got there, love.'

The carefully cultivated Cockney drawl that has characterised Shannon's speech over the last year or so is gone momentarily, and the clipped Home Counties vowels that she has so carefully hidden for so long break through. She is sobbing now.

'I can't do this. I really can't do this. Oh God. Please. You have to help me…' Shannon grips the midwife's arm as though holding on to a straw.

'You can, and you will. You've come this far, love. You're doing a grand job. Keep going. I can see the head. You're nearly there, Shannon. One big push for me, now. Go on, girl.'

Shannon turns her head away from the accusatory white walls and bright lights and focuses instead on the stars appearing in the darkening skies, framed by the tiny window of the hospital room. With every single ounce of strength left within her, she concentrates on doing this momentous thing. A child pushes another child out into the world.

It happens quickly in the end. Terry, of course, is not there to witness the birth of the daughter that might be his.

'It's a girl!'

In the peace after the delivery, Shannon experiences an unexpected rush of love for the little pink thing that lies across her, its eyes closed, a faintly furrowed expression forming across the forehead. A baby. A whole miniature human being. A brand-new little life. Shannon is awed by the whole miracle and marvel of it.

But it isn't long before a strange feeling of anti-climax overtakes her. Where are the popping champagne corks and the friends – and father – to share the miracle moment with?

Later in the evening, a couple of her flatmates do arrive – a little tipsy 'from wettin' the baby's head' before they got to the hospital. Shannon is touched that Tara and Vivi have clubbed together for the baby's first gift, a cute little poppered cotton babygrow set. More white to go with the whiteness of the room.

'Cheap an' cheerful, really – but you can't really go wrong in Asda, can you?' chuckles Tara, 'and she won't have a clue it's not designer, not at 'er age.'

'God, Shannon, she's so beautiful. Look at you now – a real mum.' Vivi is reverent in the wake of her friend's new status. 'I know it seems as though you've been pregnant, like, forever, but it's real now. She's really here. An actual baby! Can I hold her?'

All three girls are awkward as they handle the baby between them. It is the proverbial blind leading the blind.

'No, not like that. You've got to make sure you support the neck,' preaches Shannon, echoing what she has been told by the midwife.

The baby is oblivious to the clumsy passing around.

'It sleeps a lot,' Tara observes, when it is her turn to hold, not quite knowing what else to say.

'And so small. Look at them tiny fingers,' says Vivi, rubbing them between her own. 'It's like a doll.'

'*She's* like a doll,' Shannon corrects her. 'She's not an *it*.'

'She's quite pink though, in't she? Is she meant to be that pink?'

'It means she's healthy,' says Shannon, quickly. She doesn't mention that she has wondered the same thing herself but not wanted to mention it to the midwife.

'Course she is. Look at her. Beautiful, in't she?' Tara reassures her.

'Steady on, you'll be havin' one next if you start talking like that!'

'I wouldn't; it bloody hurts – a lot,' Shannon says, with all her newfound authority of a few hours in the world of motherhood.

'What was it like? Is it as bad as they say? Did they give you drugs? Did they have to stitch you up after?'

Shannon regales her wide-eyed friends with detailed descriptions of the birth. She focuses on the physical and leaves out the emotional strain she feels, but Vivi must catch something of her melancholy.

'I'll be there, like, whenever you need me,' she coos.

'Is that me or the baby?'

'You, Shan, you daft thing! But yeah, the baby as well, I s'pose. Course.' Vivi smiles at her friend.

'We can be like aunties,' Tara suggests, not to be left out of the love-in.

'Get you off to the best start in life.'

'Keep you away from the lowlifes.'

'Treat you proper.'

'Only the best for this little one.'

The grand statements of commitment come thick and fast and they truly believe them as they are being made. But the glow they leave begins to disappear almost as soon as the door closes behind Tara and Vivi – and Shannon and her baby are left alone. Time keeps on ticking by. They are in a private room. The midwife offered and it seemed like a good idea to take it, but now Shannon wishes that she was on a ward, with other new mums for company.

Shannon is faintly surprised to discover that she is bored by this tiny creature, who just doesn't seem to do very much at all. She notices that she feels claustrophobic: quietly trapped by the walls, the whiteness, the smothering needs of mothering. She has an urge, which she can't quite explain and would never admit to having, to open up the little window and throw the baby out of it. That would sort things out. She has no idea where the thought has come from. Hormones? It goes as quickly as it came, but she is unable to forget that she *had* the thought, and there is no one around to reassure her about the vulnerability that a new mother feels. The first day is so, so long. Shannon is exhausted, and wide awake. It feels a little bit like jet-lag. There is nothing to do in this maternity room. The telly only has terrestrial channels. You can pay for more but Shannon hasn't got any money. She is in pain, but it is nothing like the pain of actual childbirth. She finds herself longing for the baby to wake up for a feed. At least it would be something to do. The whole palaver of it all takes up time, and there is a sort of novelty to it. So far, anyway.

Terry doesn't make it to the hospital until nearly 24 hours later.

Shannon is buoyed up again when he eventually gets there. He arrives without warning, not even a little cryptic text, just as evening falls the next day. A small teddy bear, wrapped in cellophane and tied with a bow, nestles in the bottom of the carrier bag he throws towards her.

'Congratulations, babes!' he shouts. 'Catch!'

The relief at seeing him eliminates the barrage of recriminations Shannon has planned. But her face falls when he tells her that he is back on the run straight after tonight.

'It's not safe, darlin'. You wouldn't want to see me hurt, now, would you?'

She tries to put the reality of what that might mean out of her mind.

The new baby, oblivious to her fate being played out around her in the white hospital room, sleeps on through Terry's entrance.

'She looks like me. Do you think she looks like me? She does!' he says, staring through the glass sides of her cot. 'She's got my nose, I reckon. See, look.' He points, but makes no move to pick up his baby. Instead he winks lewdly at Shannon, and leans forward to dispense a kiss. 'Clever girl. You made another human being! Thirsty work. Cause for celebration, I reckon.' He flaps open his denim jacket so that the inside pocket and its contents are visible to the new mother.

She grins at him. 'You know me well, babe.'

They leave the baby sleeping. Shannon peeps back through the glass panel in the door.

'She sleeps for hours. It's all she does do. She won't wake yet,' Shannon advises. Together they head outside the hospital via a fire exit that Terry spotted on the way in.

'I'm not sure we should…'

'Who you tellin' what to do? Christ, you're not goin' to turn into one of them nagging slags, are you, Shan? Save it for the kid! Tell it what to do, not me.'

She, thinks Shannon. She's not a bloody object. But she knows better than to say it out loud.

Terry cracks open the tin of Stella Artois that he has bought for them to share as a loving cup. Shannon loves this rebellious side of him, and really, who is going to care that they are outside a fire exit? She giggles as she takes a too-large slurp from the little opening and liquid trickles down the side of her mouth, onto her chin.

'I'm out of practice!' Shannon laughs.

'You're dribbling! Thought it was babies that were meant to do that!' Terry licks lager off her face, while reaching into his other pocket for his baccy tin. The spliff is ready rolled. It takes him a couple of goes to light the end.

They look up above them to see the windows of Shannon's ward; and Terry, inhaling deeply, gestures a toast, as though he is the guest of honour at a fine banquet, instead of skulking out in the cold by a dirty fire exit outside the maternity wing of the hospital while on the run from the police.

'To our little girl.'

'Our little girl,' Shannon chimes back, resting her head on Terry's shoulder.

Terry reaches to take the tin can back, swapping it for the spliff.

Shannon savours the smoke curling into her mouth before drawing it down to her lungs, relishing the longed-for hit. She had really tried to cut back on the smoking and the drugs and the drinking, until the last few months when she figured that the baby was grown enough to not get damaged.

'I never want to forget this moment,' she whispers.

They pause, steadying themselves against one another beneath the stars. It is a clear night. The lager can is illuminated against the night sky, its circular red blazon bold against the white. Struck by sudden inspiration from the logo, he says, solemnly, 'You won't. Let's call her Stella.'

Shannon laughs again, at the deliciously subversive element of the idea. It's so perfect. 'Stella is a beautiful name,' she agrees, trying it out on the night air, 'Ste-lla.' She remembers, distantly, from Latin lessons at her expensive independent school, that it means 'star'.

'To Stella,' she smiles, draining the last dregs of the tin.

II

It is late morning and the bus is empty, save for a whiskered man taking up two seats at the back, and a voluminous sari-clad woman at the front. Shannon opts for somewhere in the middle, as far away from her fellow passengers as she can. She stumbles while fumbling for the right change in her purse. Not quite trusting the newborn sling that the hospital have lent her, she stays standing. There is no sign or word from Terry; he isn't answering his mobile or responding to any of her texts. She hadn't thought to bring the pram to the hospital when labour began, and she can't think of anyone else to ask for help. She just sort of assumed that she would be driven back from the hospital: there is a picture in her head of loving parents strapping their precious cargo into a car seat, but Terry doesn't even have a car at the moment so that was always going to be a fantasy, and right now she hasn't got the slightest idea where he is or what he is up to. He was totally vague on detail when he left the hospital last night, and she was exhausted – and a little bit stoned. She does at least have keys to the flat so she can let herself in even if he isn't there.

So now, here she is, on the draughty number 47, a new young mother making her way home for the first time, pretending that she knows something about what she is doing. This very ordinary thing – taking a bus ride – seems to have assumed mythic proportions: it is Stella's first journey out into the actual world. At least the rhythmic swaying and reassuring engine hum seem to be soothing the baby. Shannon, by contrast, feels far from soothed. Already her nipples are sore. Breastfeeding didn't really happen in any sort of sustained way; the idea slightly repulses her anyway. She associates it with animals. So the hospital has given her a supply of formula, with a bottle mixed for the way home just in case.

Shannon doesn't know how long it will be until Stella wakes up, but her neck is also hurting from the strange position she has been contorted into. They've done this sling up so tight, too tight; but Shannon isn't sure how to adjust it and it's safer not to try: it would be a disaster if she unravelled on the bus. She looks down at the little pink face nestled in the sling, which wrinkles into a frown as she tries to sit down. Sari woman turns round and gives Shannon a smile. Shannon tries to smile back, but it turns into a grimace as the bus handles a corner and Shannon has to hang on tight to stop Stella's little head from hitting the railing. When she casts a glance behind, the whiskery bloke ignores her, actually looking pointedly in the other direction. Shannon knows that she would have got a letchy look at the very least from someone like him just a few months before. Now she is of no interest, desexualised by the baby. She is not sure whether to be relieved or upset.

As the bus pulls back out into the road, Shannon wonders just how the hell she is going to do all of this – it doesn't seem fair to be by herself for the birth and now for this first journey. *Well, that's clearly how it's going to be, so I'm just going to have to get on with it,* she thinks. From nowhere, a vision of her own mother pops into her head. Shannon tries to push the image away, but just like in real life, she is stubborn. *No. You're not getting your hands on Stella,* she resolves. *No way.* But just for a moment it would be so nice to know that there was someone there that she could turn to.

The neatly bobbed hair, immaculately tied scarf and cashmere sweater combo that form the unmistakable image of Gill, Shannon's adopted mother, refuses to disappear. But what would Gill know anyway? They weren't capable of having their own children, so Gill has never had to do this whole baby thing herself. Shannon experiences a tiny satisfaction in having been able to do something that Gill couldn't. Gill and Simon had tried for nearly 10 years to have a baby before adopting two boys – and then Shannon. Shannon went to them when she was four years old and doesn't remember much about life before that. What she does remember is the stifling neatness of everything, borne of Simon's naval background and Gill's obsession with hygiene. And the enthusiasm that bordered on fetish with anything old, antique and historical. The house they lived in was four centuries old and flaunted its sprawling oak-beamed loveliness. Gill was desperate to scream about how cultured they all were and had *The Rhyme of the Ancient Mariner* framed in the entrance hall. They made sure that everyone knew that they had a second home in Gibraltar by having the architectural drawings on display in a cabinet by the telephone table.

It was an artificially constructed family of high achievers. Failure was not an option. Simon had medals for heroic military actions, had even conducted some dangerous rescue in peacetime that hit the headlines. The newspaper cutting from *The Telegraph* was mounted and framed in the study. Shannon's adopted brothers had both sailed through their respective red-brick universities with sporting blues. There were trophies proclaiming their glory and triumph and bloody superiority on every shelf of the immaculately preserved 17th-century country house.

Shannon isn't sure at precisely what age – or why – she made the conscious decision to reject the privilege and opportunity that a private education afforded her. Perhaps it was a result of being packed off to boarding school so young. Much was made of the ability to pay for a private education in order to support the transient nature of Simon's naval life. Shannon was sent miles away from the family home in order to be 'sorted out'. And she was – sorted out – for a long time. Swimming was her thing: it gave her the routine and the discipline that she needed. And of course, Gill and Simon lapped that up. They could not have been more supportive when Shannon showed some talent, first representing the school where the PE staff told her adoptive parents that she had 'natural ability', and then being approached by a coach for a local team. But swimming is all-consuming. By 15, the training meant five early mornings a week. It meant no highlights in her hair (she tried once – they went green). It meant no acrylic nails. What was the point? They just lifted off after a few days. And weekends were lost to competition. Once she was swimming at county level they traipsed all over the country every Saturday and Sunday. There was talk of an England trial. In good time for Olympic selection.

And then one day, it all changed. The drive was gone. She still doesn't really know what triggered it. Shannon's alarm had gone off while it was still dark one morning. In the blackness she decided that she just couldn't face the thought of the cold morning, clambering into the nylon swimsuit, the chlorine in her throat, her coach talking nineteen to the dozen about ambition and commitment. She realised that it wasn't her ambition. She pulled the duvet up higher and just thought, *fuck it*. And that was the end of the swimming. She wasn't allowed to give it up without a fight, and that's when the rows with Gill and Simon, but especially Gill – who was a sanctimonious bitch at the best of times – had really begun.

The number 47 bus lurches to a stop right outside the police station, but the pause in the journey doesn't interrupt Shannon's train of thought. Not really. Sari and Whiskers both stay on the bus, and a young lad, full of acne, bless him, gets on. Christ, it was only a few months ago, really, that she was worrying about tiny things like the condition of her skin. How different Shannon's life has become in such a short space of time. Not much more than a year, all told.

She had spent a good few months waking up and thinking 'fuck it', actually. It was easy to find friends outside of swimming club who actually had a vague idea about life. Shannon had occasionally been pissed at parties before, whenever there had been a pause in the training schedule that allowed for a break, but the drinking began in earnest when she met Vivi and Tara at a club. Real people. Not like the idiots at the private school. That's probably when she had dropped the posh girl accent, too. Shannon wanted no part of it. And it was them, Tara and Vivi, who had first introduced her to Terry. Looking back, it was fair to say that's where things had probably turned. Late nights. Trying out different drugs. Legal and illegal highs. Overdoing it. Going on the pill. Sleeping around – with Terry and some of the other men in his circle. Not coming home some nights. Then all the friction with her folks – actually with Simon more than Gill towards the end.

Shannon feels a momentary pang about what she has done to Simon. Because, of course, they had both tried to reason with her at first, together and separately. Shannon's relationship with her adopted father was much stronger. He was always more fun than Gill; perhaps that was a result of being able to swan about the world on big ships and have a life while Gill was stuck at home keeping house.

They had both tried to reset the boundaries once they had got over the swimming thing. But always at the back of Shannon's mind was the thought that they couldn't really tell her what to do. Because they weren't her *real* parents. Her birth mother was out there somewhere. Gill wasn't her mother. Simon wasn't her father. What right did they have to dictate the direction of her life in any case? She wasn't their flesh and blood. She wasn't part of this ridiculous network and competitive hierarchy in private education and their 'circles'. She didn't belong to it anyway. It wasn't her birthright. She was a fraud. An outsider. Simon became deeply frustrated and angry with her, and when the platitudes wouldn't work there were ugly scenes.

Shannon shudders as she recalls how, after a huge row, he pulled the plug of her stereo out of the wall because she couldn't hear him calling to her to turn it down. He was always actions, not words. Gill was the words. Always the bloody words: wasn't she grateful for the start she had been given? Wasn't it time that she gave something back to her poor parents who had rescued her from a life of God knows what kind of hell and misery? Didn't she understand how lucky she was? What privilege and opportunities she had been given? Did she want to drag herself back down into the gutter where she came from?

Well, she would bloody well show them that she could do 'life' on her own. Her own way. Her own rules. So, pregnant at 16, a mother at 17, she is certainly doing that. Oh yes, she is really showing Gill and Simon, she smiles, ruefully.

The engine of the bus throbs back into life with the driver's gear change, the shift in rhythm conducting Shannon's thoughts back to that final, fateful day. It has crystallised in her memory. Every sour second.

Shannon remembers that she had woken up feeling utterly nauseous, a sick sensation like never before: stabbing pains in her head and the contents of her stomach seeming to want to evacuate themselves with an urgency that she couldn't remember ever feeling before. It must have been quite some session the night before. Images like snapshots floated into her mind as she crossed the hallway to the bathroom. She didn't quite make it. The walls, adorned with the many testaments to her family's greatness – the gilt-edged certificates, mounted Grade 8 music diplomas, obligatory mortar-board posed photos clutching scroll – now had the addition of bile spatter, with the sweet stench of regurgitated cider to add to the mix. There wasn't much substance to it – it would probably wash off fine. Had she even eaten anything the night before? Shannon couldn't remember food being amongst the smorgasboard of drink and drugs that was on offer. She couldn't even have had a kebab on the way back as there were no tell-tale lumps of undigested onion or white cabbage in the vomit. Christ, she must have been steaming.

She remembers looking down at herself, wearing only pants and last night's crop top, her usually flat stomach bloated, she supposed, from all the drinking. She had managed to get herself half-undressed then, which meant she couldn't have been in that much of a state. *And at least I managed to get my shoes off*, she congratulated herself. But her head didn't, or wouldn't, stop banging, no matter how many pills she threw down her neck.

'Is that you, Shan?'

Shit! Why hadn't Gill gone out for her run, or yoga class, or whatever the hell other freaking health thing she did in the mornings? Shannon focused on the grandfather clock in the hallway next to her mother's bedroom. It took a few seconds for her eyes to settle and translate the Roman numerals into actual time. She'd slept until the afternoon. No wonder Gill was back. Shit. Shit.

'Yeah, all good,' Shannon had managed to respond, the words feeling like cotton wool filling her face.

But it wasn't all good, at all. She knew that something was very, very wrong. Young fit girls didn't suffer hangovers like this – even after a night like that. Not without something being seriously wrong. What was wrong with her?

Simon had given her a bucket to clean the hallway – like the decorated officer he was handing out duties to one of his recruits. He watched her while she tried to scrub the horror away. And she had gagged again, and thrown up into the toilet bowl this time, and then she had known. She had been on the pill, but it was easy to lose track of days when you had big nights out and slept till lunchtime or beyond. She must have missed one, or more.

She wonders now if Simon had suspected, too. He knew what having a drink was all about – cigars and port and large gins were a regular feature of his lifestyle. He might well have known that this was more than a hangover. It was Tara who jokingly suggested a pregnancy test. Shannon left home that day with a positive line on the plastic wand in her pocket, unable to reveal her condition to judgemental parents, and with only one destination available: Terry's notorious drug den.

The bus stops again. They arrive on the shabbier, less salubrious side of town, now; closer to 'home', past the tattoo parlours and fried chicken shops. Shannon eyes the graffit-ied bus shelter with its smashed pane of glass and wonders exactly what kind of world she is bringing her child into. This time Whiskers breathes beery breath across Stella's exposed forehead as he stumbles a little while moving forward to the front of the bus to get off. Shannon moves her shoulder instinctively to protect the little bundle; she stops herself from thinking 'of joy'. Because joy is very far-removed from what she's experiencing.

'Don't worry, love. Might never happen,' Whiskers calls, looking back over his shoulder.

It already has, Shannon thinks. It already has.

Anxiety overwhelms her, suddenly. She is really not sure if she can do this. Alone. She can't even balance enough to reach up to ring the bell to let the driver know that her stop is next. Perhaps she has left it too late.

Sari gives her another sweet smile. Shannon doesn't even bother to try and return it this time. It is going to take more than smiles to get her through. The bus pulls up outside the off-licence by the estate. Her stop. She only hesitates for a moment before patting the last of the money in her pocket and ducking inside the glass door instead of going straight home.

III

The flat is empty. And it is a mess: a real state. Of course it is. Shannon doesn't know why she is surprised by that. There has been no magic marigold-glove-wearing fairy to clean up while Shannon has been in hospital with Stella. What did she expect, frankly? The only visitor appears to have been Terry, judging by the overflowing ashtray and trail of tobacco across the stained and patchy carpet. Shannon inhales stale air and wrinkles her nose in disgust – a disgust that she doesn't remember feeling before. She throws open a window, but then remembers that babies need to be kept warm – warmer than adults, she knows that much – and closes it again, noticing how dirty the windows are. She wipes a finger across the grime that appears to coat the inside of the glass as well as its exterior. How do you even clean the outside, this high up? She considers the problem for a moment. It has never occurred to her before.

She looks across the room. There is a film of gunk on the coffee table. Layers of sticky spilt drink and God knows what else. It doesn't seem quite right, somehow, to have a baby here, in this chaotic environment, after the whiteness and sterility of the labour ward. Shannon resolves to clean the place up. She will start in here and have a really good go at getting it sorted. There are probably cleaning products somewhere. And if not, she can go back out and get some from the corner shop. She's good for credit in there because the owner uses and so can always knock it off what he owes Terry.

After she's had a drink to fortify her spirits.

The tinny flick of the ring-pull wakes Stella, who begins to cry. Shannon curses under her breath and takes a giant swig before easing her little pink daughter from the sling. 'I'm still sore,' she explains to the baby, 'from where you came out of me.' She points to the can. 'It's got to be a better medicine than taking pills, so don't judge me… with those little beady baby eyes!'

Shannon is conscious that she feels a strange sense of exposure in front of her daughter, even though she is a tiny baby who knows nothing whatsoever of life yet.

With Stella tucked into her arms, Shannon goes into the kitchen and starts opening doors randomly. She isn't quite sure what she is looking for, so there is no real purpose to her movements. There is no food in the house, apart from some stale cereal in the cupboard and some cup-a-soup sachets. In the fridge are silver foil cartons of leftover vindaloo. The smell is pungent and she shuts the refrigerator door fast. There is no point in looking in the freezer compartment.

That hasn't worked for ages. She is definitely going to need to go shopping.

Shannon notices that the cupboard door doesn't quite shut properly as she returns it, but hangs open, drunkenly. She is finally looking at the world with the eyes of a new mother and noticing the hazards everywhere. But she reminds herself, logically, that it will be a few months more before Stella is crawling and might get inside. There is plenty of time to sort this stuff out.

She eyes the pile of washing-up that is overflowing in the sink. Some of it has been there for weeks. That will have to stop. It really will. She takes a plate from the work surface and puts her foot out to open the kitchen bin, which is overflowing. Terry never empties it. Never even seems to notice when it has got full. She remembers now being bothered by that in the beginning, back when she had first started staying at the flat.

Stella is still crying, so Shannon doesn't try to empty the bin straight away, but balances the plate back on top of another teetering tower of unscraped plates and pots and cutlery. She's not sure where the bin-liners are kept anyway.

There are no nappies in the house, other than the handful she has come away from the hospital with. Shannon wonders idly why she didn't get more ready before she went into labour. There is the pram, standing proudly in the hallway. It 'cost a fucking arm and a leg', as Terry had so poetically put it. But no cot for Stella. Yet.

Shannon is not entirely sure that she believes in the 'yet'. That implies it *will* happen in the future. Terry had said he was 'on it', in the rare moments when she had pressed him. She hadn't liked to remind him, because it smacked too much of commitment and domesticity, things she knew that he tried to avoid. But the fact is that Stella will have to sleep somewhere. The drawers in the bedroom are roughly cot-sized. One of those will have to do, for the time being. The mattress from the pram will fit in it. She remembers studying improvisation in GCSE Drama lessons. Well, this is real improvisation, in the real world.

The cries have reached an astonishing intensity now. Did Stella cry that loudly in the hospital? Maybe it just didn't sound like it because of the other babies on the maternity wing also making a noise. What does she want? Milk, perhaps. She must need a feed already. How long was that bus ride? Shannon reaches over a grimy work surface to flick the kettle on, noticing the flabby rolls where her stomach was pressing into the Formica edge. How is it that she still looks – and feels – four or five months pregnant with the baby *outside* of her body? It doesn't seem fair. Terry isn't going to fancy her looking like this. Wherever the bloody hell he is.

Pride in what her body has done in giving birth is tainted with disgust at having had to do it all. How has she ended up here? She tries to soothe Stella. 'Yes, I want to cry, too, little one. But I'm not going to. I'm going to be bigger than that. It's no good two of us screaming the place down, is it?'

As she rocks the baby and paces up and down the few feet of uncluttered space in the flat, she remembers her first meeting with Terry: the electric charge she had felt in the knowledge that she was playing in the big league as far as men were concerned. Here was no schoolboy playing around with a packet of 10 after his homework was done; here was a stubbly, sandy-haired, muscular, tattooed *man*. The image of a weasel pops into her head, but she dismisses it. He didn't have the expensive education that she'd had, but he was worldly-wise – and that was part of his attraction. It was all Shannon could do to shield her own learning from him. She began to work harder on an affected cockney accent to mask the telling Home Counties one that she so despised. Meanwhile, Terry seemed to like the kudos that his posh bird brought, and enjoyed the often-repeated joke that she was from 'the other side of the tracks'. Her youth was another bonus that made him feel younger than his own drug-addled body did in the run-up to his 30th birthday.

Stella continues to cry, but each time Shannon takes a sip from the can, she seems to mind a little bit less about the noise. It works like a tiny inoculation.

Days pass this way.

Every one of them feels longer than the last and Shannon, alone, continually finds fresh new evidence of precisely how ill equipped she is for motherhood. Stella, for all her sleeping, manages to be incredibly demanding. She gets a rash around the mouth that Shannon doesn't like the look of, but it's easier to pretend to be out when the health visitor tries to visit, because Shannon still feels shame about the state of the place and knows that it won't look good. There just doesn't seem to be the *time* to do anything. Frankly, single parenting is exhausting. There is just no break from it.

Tara and Vivi pop round a couple of times but don't stay long. Not when Stella starts crying. It sounds so loud and accusatory and echoes round the flat. The enormity of the task of raising a child overwhelms them all. They don't seem to be 'there' for Shannon at all, in spite of what they said in the hospital, all those promises.

Terry doesn't reappear or answer his phone or respond to any of her messages. He seems to have disappeared off the face of the earth.

A knock at the front door the following week alleviates the monotony. And it isn't the health visitor. Shannon avoided Terry's mother when she was pregnant, but now has never been so pleased to see the woman. Cath lives nearby, on the same estate as her son. She is a larger-than-life woman in her late forties with a tobacco-edged laugh and red-veined cheeks that have hard lines cleft into them. Cath is the first person to have disrupted the stifling sameness of the last few days, and Shannon welcomes her in.

Embarrassed afresh by the state of the place, Shannon offers to put the kettle on 'for a brew.' Shannon knows that Cath supports her disabled husband, Terry's step-dad, and Tony, her adult son, so this is just as much a break for Cath as it is for Shannon. Shannon is glad that Cath is on her own, though. Tony really creeps Shannon out. Though he is Terry's brother and Shannon has known about his learning difficulties, still, he looks at you in that really peculiar way.

Shannon tolerates Cath smoking directly over the baby and wheezing her asthma breath over Stella's face. Shannon hopes that you can't catch asthma; but she isn't sure. As Cath folds her bulk into the sofa to sit down, Shannon is fascinated by the physicality of all that flesh. Cath's size is astounding to Shannon: she is positively rotund where Terry is rangy and wiry. It is hard to believe that they are related. Suddenly her own post-baby muffin top doesn't seem quite so bad.

'How'd it go, then?' Cath asks Shannon, gruffly, gesturing with a casual lift of the hand towards baby Stella, which Shannon understands is a reference to the birth. As though Shannon has simply been to have a tooth out. But Shannon doesn't mind really, because at least it is someone to talk to.

'Not too bad. Quite quick really, in the end.'

Throwaway sentences to cover what has been such a totally life-changing experience. But there aren't words to communicate all of that.

Over mugs of tea, Shannon learns that Cath has been in the area all her life. She grew up just a few streets away from here, and has never really been anywhere else, not even to London.

'Any sign of 'im yet?' Cath says, referring to her son. 'I 'spect the littlun has scared 'im off.' She chuckles. 'He'll be back afore long, no doubt. He'll make a good dad when 'ee gets used to the idea. Just give 'im a bit of time. You know what they're like.'

Cath has a somewhat misguided opinion of her son's qualities, and of his commitment to fatherhood, Shannon suspects. For his part, Terry has always exploited Cath for cash and for food, Shannon knows. Which could be useful. Because Stella is Cath's grandchild, after all. Flesh and blood. Probably. Shannon only hesitates a moment before she asks Cath if she can borrow a tenner. For nappies. Just until Terry gets back. Cath hands over the cash with slightly pursed lips and eyes raised to heaven.

'Thanks, Cath. Appreciate it. I'll pay it back as soon as I get myself sorted.'

Shannon tucks the money into her back pocket, gratefully. And they both know that it will likely be the last that Cath sees of it.

The off-licence is right next door to the little convenience store that sells the nappies.

It is another full week before Shannon hears from Terry. Another week of loneliness, of struggling to cope with a newborn. There is some intermittent and half-hearted cleaning (she didn't make this mess, after all) and fairly sustained drinking to get through it all, to drown all her worries and anxiety and to drown out Stella's cries. Shannon has got as far as cleaning the scum from the coffee table during an initial frenzied burst of activity, but the windows are just as grimy as they were. Not that Shannon is noticing anymore; she has solved the problem by electing not to open the curtains.

And the poor state of the flat is like a malaise that has spread to Shannon herself. Shannon hasn't got anywhere close to brushing her hair on the day that Terry finally returns. Personal hygiene has become secondary to the daily struggle for survival. She is on the sofa positioned somewhere between *A Place in the Sun* and *Cash in the Attic.* Both seem about as far removed from her current situation and possibilities as could be. A fucking place in the sun! Fat chance. There is no getting away from here, and the chance of hidden cash is laughable. Stella is wedged into the corner of the other end of the sofa in the daylight darkness. Her unfocusing eyes are not really able to process the screen images as yet, but the dulcet tones of Alistair Appleton seem to have the desired soporific effect. Shannon is yet to establish any kind of rhythm to her days. She has taken the midwife's helpful advice of 'sleeping when the baby is sleeping' quite to heart and many hours have been spent languishing on this sofa during Stella's brief existence and Shannon's time as a mother.

So Shannon's feelings at seeing Terry are all over the place. She is breathless with excitement at seeing him when he finally does turn up, and seething with rage at having been abandoned in the precious, raw few days after giving birth. He has been so out of order. She is also mortified that he has found her looking like this and curses herself for not making more of an effort. Though on the other hand he doesn't deserve it. She struggles to process her confused emotional response, though Terry's presence is at least something other than 'baby' that is finally happening to relieve the monotony in the claustrophobic flat. She is glad that he is here.

Terry throws his bag down and throws open his arms.

'Babes! How are my two favourite girls?'

Shannon is painfully aware of how unappealing and unkempt she must look in the crumpled t-shirt and leggings encrusted with baby sick. Why hadn't he at least sent a text message, or called, and given her a chance to prepare? Terry's two favourite girls aren't doing terrifically well – that much is soon apparent to the prodigal father.

'Christ! What's that smell?'

The smell, it transpires, is a signal that Stella needs her nappy changing: an activity that Shannon has been studiously putting off until she finds out the results of the middle-aged attic-scouring couple's television auction.

'Fuck's sake. Can we put a light on the situation here? Why's it so dark?'

Terry throws open the curtains theatrically to reveal a scene far removed from the tranquil domestic bliss he was expecting to return to.

'Jesus. Look at the state of you! Big night last night, was it?' he snarls sarcastically, eyeing the overflowing ashtray and remains of the six-pack that litters the table.

'Hardly, Terry. That's not fair. It's not easy looking after her, you know.' Especially without you here to help, Shannon thinks, but stops herself from saying it.

Terry sniffs the air, pointedly. 'Right. Whatever. It doesn't seem as though you're doing much "looking after", though.'

'What the hell would you know about it?'

And, just like that, what might have been a happy lovers' reunion turns into a vicious, stinging row. In her fragile emotional state, Shannon can barely respond to his taunts without bursting into tears – a 'female weakness' that she is well aware Terry despises. The fact that she knows how much he hates crying women means that she tries even harder, wills herself not to cry. To no avail. She loses the battle and the tears come readily, steadily. Stella joins in for good measure.

Terry is incensed. 'Terrific. Wailing women everywhere. Do you have any idea where I've been? Do you? I suppose you think I've been on fucking holiday?'

His personal narrative of martyrdom continues while he explains that he got picked up, eventually, by the police. Two nights in a cell while they charged him, a court appearance in a fortnight and chance of a longer custodial sentence. He's heard that this particular judge is cracking down on drugs-related crime at the moment, and will make an example of him, 'no fucking doubt'.

Stella's cries grow louder and more insistent. She still hasn't had her nappy changed.

'Oh, sod this,' snarls Terry. 'I can't even be in me own flat.'

The door slams and he is gone again.

It isn't quite the end, though. The relationship lasts for another three, intermittent, weeks, before Terry makes it clear that he is gone for good. He pays for a further month's rent on the flat – he's not a completely cold-hearted bastard – and then it is up to Shannon financially, as well as practically and emotionally.

The days grow longer and longer and more and more bleak. Stella is left alone on the sofa to cry for longer and longer periods. Something inside Shannon is broken. How is it that he can just walk out, while she is left here in this mess? This colossal, unrelenting mess of a flat – and of a life. None of it is fair. The young rebellious girl forging her own path in life is utterly shattered by the crushing realities of motherhood. There is no money. There is no support. The emotional strain is unrelenting.

The curtains are drawn during the day, but Shannon opens them at night, watches the stars, spending hours looking at the endlessness of the night sky. *Ad Astra per Aspera*. She remembers learning mottos in those Latin lessons at her independent school, a world that seems light years away. But the stars are beyond her reach. This is just too much hardship. It is too much to bear. She knows that she can never be the mother that Stella needs.

Stella is, must be, better off without her.

Stella needs a start like Shannon herself had been given in her adopted family. Somewhere nice, somewhere clean, somewhere stable. With that sort of start, perhaps Stella can do better than Shannon herself did. Shannon would give anything now for that warm, safe, sterile environment that Gill and Simon gave her. She yearns to be back inside that world rather than the flat of filth that surrounds her. What was she thinking? Why did she give it all up? What was she trying to prove? And who was she trying to prove it to? Too late, far too late, she realises how utterly stupid she has been. She has always had people around her to sort out her problems. But not now. Not now that she has really messed up. She can see that. This is not a 'problem' that can be wiped away.

A teacher once told her that Shannon would cut off her nose to spite her own face. The phrase has stuck with her. She certainly cut off her adoptive parents. And for what? They tried, in the best way that they could, with money, and privilege, to give her a better start in life. Why didn't she tell them she was pregnant? She knows why: She thought they would take her baby and try and give it a middle-class upbringing. And why would she have resented that so much? She isn't really sure, now.

Shannon has often wondered about her own birth mother, about why she had to be given up for adoption. Well, now she has an inkling. More than an inkling. She knows that right this second she would do the same in an instant. She imagines what life would be like without Stella as this yoke around her neck. She allows herself to picture an alternative lifestyle. Shannon would still be out somewhere, enjoying herself. Terry would still be around. Maybe. Though Shannon has always known in the darkest places inside her that Terry is worthless and incapable of changing – while always desperately hoping that she is somehow wrong and he will come good. What did she see in him? He is a pathetic excuse for a human being. He will never have a proper job. Drug-dealing has a clear career progression, and he is well on his way. That is no life.

What if Stella had never been born? It is an uncomfortable thought, but Shannon allows her imagination to go there. She knows that she wouldn't be sat in this minging tracksuit covered in baby puke and worse, all the while the life and youth being sucked out of her. And it isn't purely self-pity that Shannon feels. She acknowledges that Stella herself would likely be better off if she had never been born. This was no start for a baby in a tiny flat like this in a grotty neighbourhood like this one. Shannon knew exactly what sort of world Stella would be entering – who is she kidding? So this is no life for either of them. She, Shannon, would be better off dead. This is no life. This is no life for either of them. Who knew that it would be this hard?

The first few weeks of Stella's little life have been characterised by instability and neglect. It has been horrible. Shannon makes up her mind to act. To grab her life back. She tells herself – and believes – that she is doing it for Stella.

The next time Cath knocks at the door, Shannon sees her escape route and takes it.

IV

April, four years later

It is dark inside the flat.

As always, the curtains are drawn. It is never easy to know quite whether it is daytime or night-time.

And it is quiet. Very quiet.

Stella wakes up. Her first sensation is the bad pain in her tummy. She wants to eat something so much. And she is cold. Every part of her is cold from lying on the floor – without a blanket – and her elbow hurts where it has been pressed beneath her while she was sleeping. She rolls her tongue around the inside of her mouth and over her teeth, which are sticky. Her lips feel dry, but the bowl next to her is empty, not a drop of water left to drink. She shivers and reaches out towards Shark Attack, lying just a foot away from her.

'Sharky?'

She can feel his solid form, even if she can't quite see him properly in the gloom. Shark Attack is a lovely source of heat and she buries her face right into his comforting fur. In response, Sharky curls himself obligingly around Stella's little body, and then gives her bare arm a reassuring lick. They lie together like that for a moment on sodden carpet, child and pet, before the peace is shattered by a violent banging at the door. Shark Attack begins to bark continuously, his teeth showing, his hackles already risen across his back.

'Is anyone inside?' A man's voice.

A shaft of bleaching light falls across the hallway as the letterbox is raised from the outside. Stella blinks rapidly in the unexpected luminescence, and then her attention is transfixed, momentarily, by the dust motes that bounce in the alien light beam.

The knocking comes again, just as urgently.

'Is anyone there? Open up!'

Stella knows instinctively that she needs to fear this man's voice. She doesn't recognise it. It definitely isn't Terry. Or Bodger, or Phil, or Tricky. Or Uncle Bill. Who is it? Why are they here? Stella doesn't think that they should be here. Terry doesn't like it when new people come. And this voice sounds angry, or in a hurry. Perhaps Terry is in trouble. She takes a sharp intake of breath and wonders where to hide. Do they have a key? She doesn't know where the key is. Shark Attack is still barking. Stella tries to 'ssshhhh' him, but he doesn't understand.

A second, gruffer voice follows the first, and a shadow falls across the shaft from the letterbox. A pair of eyes appear.

'Oh, Jesus Christ! She's alive! Get in there, now!'

The light from the letterbox snaps shut. They have seen her. Now Stella knows it is too late to move and begins to whimper in the darkness. Her cry rises to a wail, in unison with Shark Attack's ferocious barks, creating a sinister cacophony that fills the filthy flat.

There are more footsteps, and some shuffling outside.

'One, two, THREE!'

Stella wets herself as the men in uniform break down the door and wood splinters cover the hallway.

Later, when the rozzers – she thinks that is the word that Terry uses – have mostly gone, Stella is sitting in the back of an amblemance (ambulance is a bridge too far in Stella's mouth) with some outsize clothes and a blanket around her shoulders. She has a hot chocolate in a sippy mug, which seems babyish but who cares – it tastes nice, and the people around her seem nice, too. The pain in her tummy is much better now that they have given her something to eat, and it feels good to be warm, though it isn't the same kind of warm that she gets from Sharky.

She likes the rhythmic flashing light of the amblemance, so they have left it on for her, even though they are not moving. Stella has tried to help. She told them her first name, but doesn't know what the lady in uniform means by a 'sir-name'. She doesn't understand, or can't answer, their other questions, and there are so many questions. No, Stella doesn't really know who, or where, her mummy is. She doesn't remember her mummy. She actually isn't really quite sure if she ever had one; though she knows, in a vague sort of way, that she must have done, once.

Nanny Cath is more like a mummy, but though Stella's lexicon is still very small she knows that 'nanny' doesn't mean 'mummy'. No, she has no idea how long Terry has been gone. Yesterday and tomorrow don't have any meaning. The television turned off a long time ago, she tells them. It has been dark for a 'few' sleeps, but she hasn't been counting, and she has been sharing food and water from Shark Attack's bowls since the cereal ran out. Along with some dog biscuits from the cupboard, she remembers, suddenly. It doesn't take long to get used to the funny taste. No, she doesn't know where Terry might have gone.

The door at the back of the amblemance is open and she can overhear the snatches of conversation that are going on around her outside the vehicle. Stella tries hard to piece things together.

'...alerted by the neighbours once the stream of men stopped going in and out last week...'

Those neighbours must be Shirley and Ern, the old couple next door, it was likely them who told the police. Terry is always saying they are nosy and do too much interfering.

(Stella doesn't know that Shirley and Ern cry when the police tell them that Stella was asleep, not dead, are sorry for not getting involved sooner, and do everything that they can to answer the police questions.)

'…totally naked, and surrounded by dog shit and empty beer cans and rotting food.'

Shark Attack couldn't help pooing and doing his business. Stella didn't have the key to let him go out and the front door was locked. When you have to go, you have to go. Everyone knows that.

'…utterly foul. Never seen anything quite like it in all my days…'

'…smeared in faeces…'

Stella isn't quite sure what feeces are. Like faces, maybe?

'…pitiful…'

'…starving. So thin. Looks like her little arms would snap…'

Stella holds her arms out in front of her, rolling up the sleeves on the big jumper. She feels the white skin, putting pressure at different points along her wrist, feeling all the way up to her shoulder. Are they still talking about her? Her arms feel ok. Will they really break?

'Snap' is such a horrible word.

'…tell you something, he wants taking out and shooting. How can you abandon a little kid like that?'

Shooting? Like in the games on the PlayStation. Stella has watched lots of shooting on the laps of Terry and his friends. It is funny. Terry's friends laugh and shout at shooting. Shooting means that everyone is happy. Blood and dying is fun.

'Total darkness. No wonder she's so pale, poor thing…'

'No idea how long she was on her own like that?'

'…maybe as much as a week, judging by the state – and stench of the place…'

'…nothing in the meter. Electricity ran out before the weekend…'

'And nothing but a pit bull terrier for company…'

That's Shark Attack. He is definitely a pit-ball. As well as a dog. Pit-ball is a breed.

'…like something out of a warped city version of *The Jungle Book*…'

'She's surely old enough to be going to school…'

'…but no application for a school place on the local council register…'

She switches off when she hears the words 'drugs' and 'prison.' She has heard those plenty. She links them together. She knows that is where Terry was when she first stayed with Nanny Cath, in the drugs-prison. But she doesn't know much about the rest of her history. Or at least only has a very sketchy idea. She can't know that Nanny Cath is the matriarch of the family who has tried to hold it all together, initially with the very best of intentions, for a little girl that nobody seems to want. Stella is flesh and blood after all. And it was Nanny Cath who was left quite literally holding the baby when Shannon fled.

But Nanny Cath had too many other dependants, and a string of other people in the house, to really have room for Stella and to be able to look after her properly. Stella doesn't fully understand that she has been part of an informal kinship care arrangement, passed around from one family member to another 'to do a little stint to help Terry' since her mother ran away a few weeks after Stella was born.

After Nanny Cath, Stella stayed with Nanny Cath's sister for a while and then one of Nanny Cath's children who had a baby. She remembers that. That baby cried a lot. A lot. That baby can't have known that crying was bad. Stella had tried to tell it – to protect it – but it hadn't made any difference.

Then there was another man, Uncle Bill; she remembers nice food at Uncle Bill's. Then back to Nanny Cath. So Stella is very used to moving around and staying somewhere different and the amblemance seems as good a place as any right now. It would be quite nice to stay in here.

Stella is too young to know that Nanny Cath has done her very best to keep Stella out of the formal care system for as long as she could. A deep mistrust of any outsiders interfering 'in her private business' runs deep in the family.

But when Cath ran out of family to foist Stella onto, she went for a formal kinship arrangement herself with the local authority in order to get the money: the foster care allowance. The authority was only too happy to give the allowance since the kinship care option was, and still is, significantly cheaper than the cost and bureaucracy of placing a child in care. Cath put on a good show for the authorities and said all the right things to get the extra £200 in allowances – a great deal of money for someone in her position.

But when Terry came back out of prison, Nanny Cath passed Stella back to him, neglecting to tell the authorities about the situation in order to keep on claiming the allowance. As far as Cath was concerned, she was entitled to some financial comeback after all she had been through. And it was never going to make up for all the hard work that she had put into those first couple of years when the flighty mother ran off and left her son, her Terry, as a struggling single parent. It doesn't cross Cath's mind that she has, in fact, committed a crime, because the human need for payback is important. She deserves that money. And nobody from the authorities ever checks properly anyway, so what's the harm?

The harm is that Terry's care, or what passes for it, has had disastrous consequences for a helpless child, and has ultimately led to Stella lying abandoned, naked and starving in a pool of human and dog excrement for a string of dark days.

But right now, for Stella, it is an exciting day. This tiny, too-pale, too-thin, elfin girl is glad to see all of these people and likes the shiny lights and buttons that switch on and off inside the amblemance: they look like some of the toys she has seen on television. But she doesn't really know what all the fuss is about. Though maybe daddy *had* been gone for a bit longer than usual. Everyone has been gone for a very long time. It was so quiet inside the flat. The only noises came from Shark Attack. And it was very, very dark. It is bright outside the windows here. Perhaps they will let her go outside into that sunny daylight. Stella shivers again, even though she is warm now.

'Where's Sharky?' Stella asks the uniform lady. She hasn't heard him bark for a little while now. She feels a little bit lost without Sharky to hold on to. The uniform lady swallows and asks Stella if she would like more hot chocolate.

'Where's Terry?' she asks the uniform lady when the second hot chocolate is finished. There is no answer to that question, either; uniform lady seems to stare into the space above Stella's head, but Stella does get a lollipop. Stella tries to think about other things she could ask. It seems you get rewarded if you think of a good question.

'Where's Nanny Cath?'

The uniform lady is provoked into a response. She does seem more interested in finding out about Nanny Cath, but Stella can't tell her where Nanny Cath lives. Nanny Cath is supposed to have one of these 'sir-names' too, but Stella isn't sure what it is either, so she changes the subject.

'Where's the PlayStation? Can I play a game?'

At this the uniform lady gives Stella another sad look and pulls the blanket up tighter around her. No need. Stella couldn't be any warmer. This is a lovely blanket. She wonders if she can keep it. In a sudden impulse she throws her arms around the uniform lady, who smells lovely and… clean, but the uniform lady doesn't seem to like it very much and unpeels them. Stella is not to know that the uniform lady is beside herself and wants nothing more than to cuddle this brave little girl, but is simply acting in accordance with her training and understanding of safe care.

'How about we try to find your mum, love?'

Stella gives an involuntary shiver in spite of the snuggly warmth.

V

June

In the end, it doesn't take that long for Shannon to be found. She is discovered living a new life in another city, but not too far away as the crow flies. It happens to fall under the jurisdiction of a different local authority – which later makes tracking a fragile paperwork trail more complex – but a mixture of guilt, and curiosity, and the fact that she is a few years older and might be able to deal with things a bit better now, helps persuade Shannon that it is time to resume motherhood duties. Shannon very deliberately cut all ties with Terry when she left, deleted and blocked his number from her phone. She had been determined to make a fresh start.

Now that she has been travelling (Gill and Simon paid for a round-the-world ticket; there was a short-lived reunion of sorts, and they are still none the wiser about the existence of a grandchild), she feels that she has at least managed to get some of her youth back, a gap year of sorts. It was a hedonistic time. Thailand was full-on, with its full-moon parties and raves, and in India she draped herself in beads and braids and took plenty of time to try and 'find herself' through exploring alternative cultures, often with the help of some mind-bending substances.

But of course Shannon never quite stopped wondering what happened to the little baby she gave life to. Even while backpacking around Australia, thousands of miles away from her worries on the other side of the world, and as far away from her troubles as she could possibly run, Stella was never very far from her mind, especially beneath the stars in an alien night sky. She can't ever look up at the stars without thinking about Stella. The image of those beady baby eyes have always haunted Shannon – especially at moments when she tries to get out of her mind to forget. That is when the memories of the birth and of the tiny baby are most ferocious and unstoppable.

She had hoped that Stella was having a better life. She had told herself repeatedly that Cath and Terry would have sorted it out between them. Cath was good with kids. She knew what she was doing; she would have made things right. She knew what she was doing because she'd had plenty of experience of families, had raised enough of her own. Unlike Shannon herself, who knew nothing back then. The letter and the visit from social services come out of the blue, but they aren't accusatory. The social worker tells Shannon that she understands why Shannon couldn't cope as such a young mother. It's very common, and she didn't have the right support in place. But a four-year-old is much less demanding than a baby and Stella will be going to school soon. Shannon makes up her mind to get involved again almost straight away.

The social worker is very persuasive, giving her a hard sell of sorts and smoothing over the fact that Shannon has no relationship whatsoever with the baby she abandoned. Instead they focus on the positives: it is right that a child should be with its birth parent, blood is thicker than water, a loving home is what a child needs. The social worker focuses on the fact that Shannon is older and wiser now and understands much more about the world than she did as a teenager. What is not mentioned is the fact that Shannon has only just turned 21, and has not really matured very much over the intervening years. What is also not mentioned is the nationwide shortage of foster carers and money at the time and the money-saving appeal of a policy to get children back home to family. Shannon drinks it in.

Now estranged from Gill and Simon once more, after they found out about the drugs, it might now be time to do this properly, Shannon thinks. To face up to her responsibilities. To get her life back on track and make something of it, to make up for lost years without her daughter. With the support of the social workers, while Stella is placed in a temporary foster home, Shannon gets a little room ready for her daughter and prepares to welcome her. Stella will be five in October and will therefore be starting school after the summer. They have a few months to get to know each other. Shannon will have to drop the shifts she does at the supermarket but she can pick them up again when Stella is at school. She had it all worked out.

And now is the important time in Stella's life, anyway. Stella wouldn't be able to remember much about those first few years, when she was just a baby. Now that she is a walking, talking little person, it is exactly the right time for a fresh start. Shannon herself doesn't remember much of her own life before the age of about six or seven, she doesn't remember anything of her own birth family or foster care before she was adopted by Gill and Simon, so how important can it be?

Shannon is nervous. But she is really determined to get her chaotic life under control. This time. Once Stella's room is sorted she has a really good go at cleaning the rest of the flat. Windows, carpets, everything. It feels good to get it all sorted, and to do it by herself without relying on anyone else. She buys new stuff for the kitchen. Like in a proper house. All drug paraphernalia is disposed of, for now. That shouldn't be around a child. The one-night stands *will* stop. That would also be so inappropriate with a child in the next room. One-night stands is a euphemism, really. People don't usually pay money for one-night stands. But that is the way that Shannon justifies the extra income to herself. Prostitution is not a word that she allows herself to use. And she won't need to do it anymore anyway: the social worker has emphasised the financial support that she will get, and helped set up the other benefits, the family allowance. So Shannon will have a bit more money coming in. A four-year-old can't be that expensive to keep.

Stella's arrival day soon comes round. Shannon jokes with friends (who are aghast at the revelation of her secret background, but isn't it grown-up, having a child!) and together they celebrate her last hours of 'freedom' with a big clubbing night. It ends in a 4am kitchen disco, with a house full of hangers-on to celebrate the imminent arrival, but it isn't too hard to clear up and hide the evidence, ready for Stella's arrival, even with a throbbing head. Just a little bit of amphetamine is all it takes, to blow the cobwebs out. Not enough that it will show. Just a tiny hit to take the hangover – and the anxiety – away. To make Shannon feel a bit better: about life, the universe and everything in it, including being a mother again.

Walking up the stone steps to the flat that Shannon rents, Stella grips the hand of Grey Lady. Grey Lady isn't really grey, but her suit is. She smells of tobacco and mints. And Grey Lady did say what her name was but Stella has heard so many names over the last few weeks that she has stopped trying to remember them all. Many of them she never sees again anyway. So it is easier to latch onto a colour or a characteristic of each person. The nice amblemance (ambulance remains too much of a mouth-ful, though the flashing lights and buttons will forever be

54

etched onto Stella's memory) uniform lady with the hot chocolate and the lollipops was soon gone, and since then it has been a succession of different adults and different places with different beds to sleep in. Some of the adults have uniforms, some not. Some use their first name, some use Mr or Mrs and a surname. Stella has found out what that means now, but it is still easier not to learn them. Classifying people by the way that they look is much more straightforward than by name.

Stella isn't really nervous this morning, though everyone is making out that this is a very important day and seems obsessed with 'fresh starts'. She is a little curious about meeting her mummy today, but 'mummy' itself is a sort of abstract concept. Stella can't imagine or conjure a real face to the idea of mummy. Maybe she will be like the amblemance lady and have lollipops. But the amblemance lady was also sad for some reason; Stella hopes that her mummy will be happy. She wonders if her happy mummy has a dog. Stella is really missing Shark Attack, thus far responsible for the most consistent displays of love and affection in Stella's short little life. Perhaps they can find Shark Attack and bring him to live with them. She will ask.

Stella grips Grey Lady's hand a little more tightly after they ring the doorbell.

It isn't just the hangover that causes Shannon's surprise at the appearance of the little fairy child holding the hand of the social worker on her doorstep. It is Stella's appearance. Is that really her, thinks Shannon. She still looks so little. And breakable. Four-year-olds are bigger and more robust than that, surely? She wasn't expecting her still to be so small. And those big, wide, searching, seeing eyes – way too large for her face – scare Shannon a little bit. She is transported back to those beady eyes that she found so startling in the beginning. Stella seems… not quite real, not quite of this world.

Shannon doesn't really know what to say.

'Hello… darling. Stella. It's nice to meet—' she corrects herself, 'to… see you. Come to… Mummy.' Shannon swallows the word that sounds unnatural in her throat. She never really used it herself as a child. Gill was always 'Gill' or sometimes 'mother', but never 'mummy' when Shannon was little. Simon and Gill were clear from the start that each of the children were adopted.

When Stella doesn't answer straight away, Shannon tries a different tactic and holds out her hands to welcome her; but the strange little girl seems reluctant to let go of Grey Lady. Shannon puts her hands back to her sides, nervously, and licks round the edges of her mouth to stop the dryness. What was she thinking staying out so late and carrying on back at the flat after? She should have had a nice early night to be on top form for this moment.

She flinches a little under Stella's searching gaze. It is almost as if Stella knows that Shannon has a hangover. She is not to know that Stella is seeking the defining characteristic. God, those bloody eyes! *Stop looking at me,* Shannon thinks. It feels as though Stella is looking into her. Right through her, as though unravelling all of Shannon's flaws and laying them bare.

But a child isn't capable of doing that. It must be the speed talking. That probably wasn't a very good idea, either. Jesus, she is already making a mess of this. Shannon refocuses, turns her attention to the social worker, all in grey. What is that about? Not very cheery for children. Very off-putting. It is all very awkward on the doorstep. Shannon remembers just in time to invite them in and offer some coffee to the woman in grey.

Stella peers up at this woman who is her mother. She does a quick assessment. This one is definitely not like the suity-uniform people of her recent life. She is more like the ones who used to visit her daddy at the other flat. At the home flat. This lady's tracksuit looks soft but her eyes look hard, and wobbly at the same time. And...wild. She is a Wild Lady. Stella doesn't want to be left here with a Wild Lady. She doesn't want to go back to the old life. She bursts into tears. She has learned that it helps, these days. It never used to.

Shit, thinks Shannon. What an utter cock-up she has already made of everything. Again. The social worker is reassuring. It is an 'emotional day' for everyone. This kind of reaction is entirely normal. Things are bound to be a bit

57

strange at first. They troop into the flat and Shannon shows them into the sitting room.

She forgets that she has already offered coffee, and asks again.

'Would you like a drink?'

She means the social worker, but it is a small voice that answers first.

'Can I have some milk, please?'

Milk. She didn't think of that. For a moment she wonders if she should have bought bottles and formula and feels wholly inadequate again. Then she takes hold of herself and remembers that it's only babies that drink milk like that. Kids like actual milk. From cartons. Shannon realises that she only has skimmed in the fridge. She has bought squash to drink – because that's what you give children, isn't it? – and some fizzy stuff in case she doesn't like squash, but she didn't think of milk. Can you even give children skimmed milk? She finds a glass. Is Stella too young for an actual glass, though? What if she smashes it? Think. Bang some cupboard doors. That will help. Eventually Shannon discovers a plastic beaker at the back of one of the cupboards. God knows why it is there or what is was used for before. She blows out the dust and whatever else it is that is nestling in the bottom, slops the milk in to it and stirs an instant coffee into a mug for the grey lady. She notices the dark stains on the outside of the mug, but it is the cleanest one that she has.

Shannon could murder a cigarette, but it's probably

not a good idea in front of the kid. Her kid. Shannon has to keep reminding herself of that. Why is it all so difficult? She brings the drinks through from the kitchen to where the woman in grey is trying to interest Stella in some toys in the corner. Shannon has been collecting them from friends and charity shops since she knew that Stella was coming.

Stella takes a sip of her drink and her features reformulate into a little frown.

'What's wrong?' asks Shannon.

Very quietly, almost in a whisper, Stella says, 'Can I have another glass of milk please…' There is a slight pause. 'This tastes like smoke?'

Shannon already feels as though she can't seem to do anything right. She returns to fetch the glass and makes conversation with the woman in grey. Stella still doesn't seem very interested in the toys, but 'she has a lot going on, emotionally, so don't worry', the social worker explains. She keeps on talking about Stella needing time for 'processing' and says that will explain any unusual behaviours that Shannon might observe over the next few days. Shannon has no idea how she will get through the next few hours, let alone days.

Shannon wonders what Stella has been up to for the last few years. All children like playing with toys, don't they? And she picked the doll out specially, that Stella now refuses to pick up. A sweat forms on Shannon's top lip. She feels hot and then quickly cold. It is part hangover, yes, but part something else, too: something bigger and more overwhelming than

Shannon can name. Something that threatens to engulf her entirely. It is the realisation that there is this, and only this. She, Shannon, and a child that is somehow no longer *her* child. Never really was her child, she understands now. The realisation leaves her hollow. She has been here once before and failed. She is going to fail again. How do other people manage it?

After some forms and signatures and more reassurances, the woman in grey disappears. Shannon feels the absurd urge to throw her arms around the stranger, to cling onto her and not let go. *Don't leave me,* she thinks. *Don't leave me here on my own with her.* And already the strangling panic that she had forgotten about from when Stella was a tiny baby has begun to return. *I don't know how to do this.*

The day stretches out ahead of Shannon. The flat feels much smaller with Stella in it. More claustrophobic. It is as though the walls have crept in a few inches when she wasn't looking. The furniture that was perfectly good this morning now looks as though it doesn't fit; it might spill out of itself or burst from its place. Shannon realises that she too feels like that: as though she no longer fits; that something might burst out of her. She tries hard to smother those feelings.

What to do? Shannon wonders if Stella can read. She doesn't have any books in the house, but finds something on her phone. Stella seems more interested in the phone than the story, so Shannon hands it over, only too happy to allow Stella the distraction.

The kid, Shannon realises, has hardly spoken. She just reaches out for things rather than asking for them. Shannon is at a loss for making conversation as everything she begins with leads to a dead end. She doesn't want to mention Terry – daddy – that would be awkward for both of them. So conversation is awkward and stilted. The whole day is awkward. Stella only nods politely when she is shown her room, and says 'thank you'. She has nice manners, at least, but Shannon just doesn't know what to *do* with her.

Shannon is going to need a lot of help in order to do this, she realises. But she doesn't know where it is going to come from. None of her friends have children. They are all busy celebrating 21st birthdays. It's a big year for parties. Shannon wonders how early you can put a pre-schooler to bed. Quite early, she hopes. She also feels a strange desire to get in touch with Terry again, now that Stella is right here in the flat. She slightly regrets deleting and blocking his number, but actually, there are enough people whose number she still does have that would know how to get hold of him.

She picks up the doll again, the one that she has chosen specially. She wiggles the arms to make it wave goodnight to Stella, but somehow the gesture is grotesque. The doll has more life, more animation in her rigid plastic figure and limbs than Shannon does. And Stella sees it all.

VI

September

Today is the day. It could not have come soon enough.

Shannon has mixed feelings about Stella starting school. On the one hand she will be thankful for the break: six whole hours a day that she will get back to herself. It's exhausting being with a four-year-old all day, and Shannon's mates are getting fed up with a kid hanging around all the time, too.

There's also the matter of free meals for all reception children, which will save her a few quid each week. Christ, kids are expensive to feed. (She doesn't even want to think about the eye-watering sums of money she has had to fork out for school uniform. Why do they need a uniform at all in reception class? Shannon has no idea. It's not like they're going to do actual work, is it? To Shannon's mind, it's more of a glorified nursery, or playschool.)

But on the other hand, well, school represents another institution with the ability to meddle and interfere. Shannon has coached Stella carefully about what she is and isn't allowed to say beyond the walls of their flat, and has rehearsed responses to any potentially leading questions that she has anticipated. Because Shannon frequently leaves Stella alone, or with friends, or even with friends of Terry – but they are not carefully vetted, not the friends that a less desperate mother would leave a little girl with, and so Shannon could really do with some of what goes on not getting out into the open. Shannon, while welcoming the time to herself that Stella being at school will mean, perceives school as a potentially dangerous place.

But here they are on day one. They missed the 'familiarisation day' back in July so this is Stella's – and Shannon's – first proper experience other than an informal visit last week that actually felt more like an interview. The reception teacher, Mrs Griffiths, is an ancient old crone with dodgy dyed hair to cover the grey and an inability to apply her makeup. What galls Shannon the most, though, is that she actually had the cheek to suggest a home visit before Stella started at the school.

'It helps us to get to know you and your family set-up, and opens up that home-school dialogue.'

Yeah, right. Home-school dialogue, my arse. An opportunity to poke your nose in where it isn't wanted, is what Shannon actually thinks. Taking liberties like inviting yourself into someone's home like that can't actually be legal, surely? So Shannon has been evasive so far, figuring that they'll let it drop after a few weeks. There will be no need for a home visit once Stella has settled into school.

Shannon has learned how to play the games and make all the right noises to keep the current social worker happy and off her back (not Grey Lady, she didn't last five minutes, she was just the supervising officer tasked with doing the handover; she couldn't wait to leave. Stella was given a new social worker after that, because moving in with Shannon meant that Stella had moved into a new district and was assigned to a different local authority, and because she was now living with her mum all responsibility passed to a different team).

This new social worker initially began visiting weekly to make sure that things were going well, and helped Shannon with the forms to register Stella for a late application to the local primary school. Content that Shannon is now 'meeting all her parenting expectations' this social worker has, thankfully, taken a step back and the visits and interference have dropped right off. Others have told Shannon that if you keep your head down and don't cause trouble then they don't bother you. It's just a question of staying off their radar, never asking questions and never giving them anything to chew on. So Shannon has been careful to not actually say 'no' to the visit, just not allowed herself to be pushed into an actual date for it to happen. She is becoming much more adept at this stuff. In learning the rules for playing the system, she has discovered that most social workers just want to get home and not have more work.

Over the few months that Stella has been back in her care, Shannon has tried hard to be the mother that Stella needs, but being at home with a disconcertingly perceptive little girl is frustrating. One who, to all intents and purposes, is a stranger. She has had a stranger in her home for all this time. The summer was long and hot and Shannon quickly felt fed up with the repetition and drudgery of it all. On one level this school start date couldn't come quickly enough.

In the playground, some of the other mums are brandishing tissues flamboyantly, and making a big show of the emotional strain of separation from their offspring. Already the imposing school gates have begun to feel like a threat for Shannon. She has a sense of the other mums and dads judging her in their huddles as they stand behind their flash buggies chatting. She is much younger than the majority of them and a post-stoned paranoia kicks in. Shannon feels like she can't get out of there quick enough. It is going to be her first properly child-free day in nearly three months and she has arranged to meet up with friends and go up town, like the old days, to celebrate. Stella will be fine at school. She is a polite, compliant little kid.

Away from Stella, Shannon loses track of time, such is the novelty of freedom after weeks of being shackled to a kid – and she is just the tiniest bit late for pick-up. She may also have had a slightly extended lunch session, but Christ, she's allowed to enjoy herself, surely? She turns up to an empty playground, only Stella's face peering forlornly through the railings and Mrs Griffiths behind telling her that 'everything is going to be alright, mummy is sure to be here soon.'

To Shannon she says, 'School actually finishes at 3.15 in the afternoon. Perhaps you weren't aware…'

Shannon feels as though she is back at school herself, and snatches up Stella's hand, muttering gruff thanks as they flee the school site. It's not much past four. What are they, the time-police?

Somehow, after that, it becomes easier to be late. Both for dropping off and for collecting. The routine is hard when you have had none. And sometimes it's easier not to go in the building, so as not to have to deal with the accusatory, judgemental stares from the receptionist. The headteacher, as well as Mrs Griffiths, seems to have it in for Shannon, so she avoids both of them at all costs. How do these people not understand how difficult it is to get a kid to put their shoes on in the morning, and just leave the house? So, if they are *really* late then it is just easier, and less stressful all round, not to go in at all. And Shannon hasn't really ingratiated herself with the other mums who gather in tribes at the school gates or stand expectantly in the playground in the afternoon, so she is often deliberately late to pick-up, too, because it is easier than making small talk, or feeling isolated. They are all much older than her for one thing. Shannon knows that their lives are very different from her own. They have the aura of Gill and Simon, of money and of nice middle-class homes. She has nothing in common with any of these people other than the fact that they all have children in reception class.

One of them, with a plum stuck firmly in her mouth, had the cheek to try to tell Shannon that it wasn't appropriate to be seen smoking outside the school gates. *Outside* the gates. She wouldn't do it on the playground, obviously, but it was still a free country the last time she looked and no-one should be able to tell her what she can and can't do in the open air! Seriously, who do these people think they are?

By the time that Stella has been at school for nearly seven weeks – a whole half term – she has technically only attended half of the days that she should. The school are quick to report their concerns to the local authority. An Education Welfare Officer, EWO, from the school gets involved and tries to come round. Why do the school continually want to send someone round to her house? It is such an imposition. Who do they think they are?

Shannon is right to be concerned about the headteacher, Mrs March: she really is an interfering old busybody who does not take 'no' for an answer, but follows things up independently, keeps records diligently and is relentless in her approaches to social services. She phones the police herself when the absences continue into the second half term, and only increase after Christmas. She records every time that Shannon is late to collect Stella. Sometimes it's by a couple of hours. Shannon wonders how this woman has nothing better to do than write all of this down. They don't seem particularly interested in how Stella is getting on at school, in her actual education – just how Shannon is doing as a mother.

They even make a fuss when Stella doesn't have her book bag one day because she stayed with Terry at the weekend and Terry forgot to bring it back when he brought her to school. An easy mistake. There must be other families where the parents are separated, and that sort of thing happens, surely? Though Shannon has been getting on better with Terry these days, since she has said 'yes' to some of his demands. But it's easier not to think about that.

As far as the school is concerned, there are plenty of other signs that all is not well. Mrs March adds copious notes to her careful log, noting every bruise and some disturbing behaviour when Stella gets changed for PE. She adds details about when Shannon seems particularly under the influence of drugs or alcohol, it isn't always possible to tell. The accusations mount up.

Stella is swiftly taken into care following an unannounced home visit at the start of the third term of her school career. The police and two child protection social workers remove Stella from Shannon's chaotic and grubby life. In many ways, it is a relief for Shannon. She can't be bothered to fight anymore, to pretend that things are ok.

Stella has been with her mother for less than a year, this time round.

Later, that will seem like a blessing.

Part Two:

Old Habits Die Hard

Chapter 1

JUNE, Louise.

The phone rings. Annoyingly, just as I am standing on top of a stool reaching up for a cookbook that's sitting right in the farthest corner of the top shelf.

I've just finished clearing up after the children's dinner. The children generally eat first on a school day, before Lloyd and me, as they are usually starving when they get in. To complicate the staggered dining arrangements, our current foster child, Lily, has recently announced her decision to become a vegetarian, though the only vegetarian components she is currently willing to accept are strawberries and sweetcorn. My birth sons are confirmed carnivores, and largely unwilling to even experiment with a vegetarian diet. Meals without meat aren't proper meals, apparently. Meal preparation has therefore increased exponentially: I have gone from making one dish an evening to serve everyone, to having to create two entirely separate meals.

Whenever we have visitors they are always astonished

that I prepare several versions – restaurant-style. I keep hearing platitudes like, 'oh, that must be such hard work' or the one that really annoys me: 'we all eat together and my children eat *everything*. The focus isn't on the food, it's a time to share news.' That may be, but not in a house where there are dinners with foster children whose only control over their lives might be their food. To be fair, I am happily amazed at how much easier it is to be vegetarian and vegan nowadays, compared to when I was a vegan back in the 80s. Back then everything I ate was brown and sloppy and usually came on toast or with rice. Now there are far more innovative options. This, however, is failing to satisfy Lily, who has been enjoying *some* of the dishes I have conjured up, just not the bits with *actual vegetables* in them. The not-liking of vegetables creates something of a challenge, even for my creative brain, and menu-planning is far from straightforward. Still, as with most things in life, I am determined not to be beaten.

This particular evening, Lily and I have been having a familiar, and tonight momentarily heated, discussion.

'Chips. I'll eat those. Chips are vegetables.'

There's the tiniest hint of a tipped 'r' in Lily's speech, all that's left of the Scottish accent that she arrived with.

'We-ll, no, chips aren't vegetables. Not exactly…'

'They come from potatoes. Potatoes are vegetables. They provide important nutrition. Things like potassium and Vitamin C.'

'You're right. Potatoes are technically a vegetable, yes. But in terms of nutrition, they are considered more of a starchy carbohydrate. They don't count towards your five a day. And Chips. Fried. In. Oil…' (My punctuation is intended to be defining, and mask my increasing exasperation.) 'Well, they *definitely* don't count as vegetables.'

Lily, who has lived with us now for more than six years, has become very much part of the clan. It's fair to say that before she came into our care Lily had very little in the way of conventional boundaries. She may have lost the accent in that time, but fighting for her place in a family of nine before she came to us means that she is still very much a feisty young woman – and I am working hard to channel her hot temperament into something positive and productive.

As an ex-looked-after-child myself, and as a woman, I know that temper and tenacity will be necessary to survive: but there is still a great deal of work to do with Lily in order for her to be able to control these aspects of her personality. I've been trying hard to teach her to 'pick her fights': she has a tendency to want to always be right and can still feel threatened and vulnerable when she is not. If she is criticised she quickly becomes defensive. So negotiating tricky areas around food, alongside her burgeoning political awareness about its production, is delicate work. It would be easy to let her have her way, but my job, as I keep reminding her, is to help her become a good person who can live and work effectively with others.

We are definitely making progress.

She used to strop off, slam doors, and pull her room

apart in protest; but now she's learning to think through her arguments in a rational way and not see everything as an opportunity for conflict. She is learning that sometimes she just has to let things go. It has taken five years of constant hard work to help her feel safe enough to start to believe that. I am absolutely certain that one day she is going to get there fully, and she will be amazing. But her newfound tendency towards 'reasoning' with me is proving just as exhausting and frustrating, and Lily isn't going to let this one drop. She is adamant that vegetables will not be part of her vegetarian diet. I suspect that her aversion is some sort of a hangover from her earlier life of neglect.

'If it's protein that you're worried about, then I can get all the protein I need from eggs. I don't need vegetables to live,' she explains, with all the intensity, conviction and absolute certainty of early adolescence.

'But have you ever heard of a *vegetarian* who didn't eat *vegetables*? Seriously. There's a clue in the name.'

The boys, Jackson and Vincent, my birth sons, are well used to this argument rolling back and forth between us by now. Lily has served, and I have returned. There is some eye-rolling and a request to leave the table. They aren't stupid: if mum is distracted enough by the argument then this could become a prime opportunity to sneak extra crisps and sweets into their pockets and make their merry way to the safety of their rooms in order to play on their devices and consume a second, unhealthier supper than the one they have just eaten.

Before they evaporate into virtual worlds, I pause the discussion with Lily in order to ask if they have any homework.

Together they chant 'NO!'

I suspect some manipulation of the truth here – the response has been chorused too quickly, but I will remember to check in a bit.

Meanwhile, Lily is determined to win her argument about why lentils are in fact the devil's work and chips should form the staple of her diet.

'And how can I eat vegetables when I don't actually even like them? Whereas, I do very much like chips.'

She folds her arms, believing this to be game, set and match.

I, however, have left nothing behind in the locker room. 'Well, how about we pick some new vegetables and some new recipes? You haven't tried every vegetable on the planet, so how do you know that you don't like all of them?'

I have a cunning plan to get her to try and experiment with some new tastes by tempting her with gorgeous photographs of plates of colourful vegetarian delights. It's while I am precariously balanced on the chair reaching up towards a copy of a very good vegetarian recipe book that my mobile goes.

I recognise the number of the placements team.

Our conversation is brief. I hang up and Lily gives me an

expectant look. All thoughts of food are gone.

'Child?'

I nod.

Lily knows, perhaps more than any of us, that when there is a call like that, it is important. After all, it was the reality of her own experience, once. She was the 'child' about to arrive here – in her case, in a new country as well as a new family. She will do everything she can to make another child feel welcome, whatever her views on the relative merits of chips and lentils.

The atmosphere becomes focused in a very different way as we collectively start the family process of receiving a referral.

The first thing I must do is find Lloyd to break the news. He is working in his studio on a new catalogue for an old client who over the years has become a family friend. They are on Facetime, chatting through details of the layout of the catalogue when I walk in and mouth 'emergency.' I wave at his client and explain that there is a five-year-old girl on her way to us. Actually, I then backtrack and 'ask' Lloyd if it's okay that we take her, though he knows as well as I do that neither of us is capable of saying 'no' as long as the circumstances are right in our own family at the time.

Lloyd's client, who knows that we foster, and also has four children of her own, immediately says, 'Lloyd, you go. No hurry on the layout. We can come back to this.' There is something beautiful about being connected to good people who genuinely care and understand how important fostering is, even in the midst of the commercial world of business deadlines.

'Her name is Stella,' I tell him as he finishes the call. 'Nice name, don't you think? She was in an emergency placement last night but it was,' and here the contact on the placements team had paused for a fraction of a second, but long enough for me to understand the nuance, 'not ideal.' Already I feel sorry for this little girl and the problematic disruptions she has experienced, just to get as far as us. 'Not ideal', the phrase the woman on the phone used, will, inevitably, be euphemistic.

'Her carer had booked a holiday; the flight is today.' I know this particular foster carer of old: she is wonderful and only does emergency foster placements, but like all of us, she needs that holiday. Lloyd shrugs his shoulders. He knows that it is a done deal. We, more than anyone, understand. We have been in that position ourselves. This carer will have taken Stella under duress, knowing that the timing wasn't right because she was about to go on holiday and would have to leave her almost immediately, meaning that now the poor little girl might have to go through the trauma of meeting several families in a short space of time. Being in care at the age of five means that a good deal of trauma is likely to have already happened. Whatever has gone on before in her short little life, she will now have had an additional traumatic few days. Idioms about raining and pouring are exchanged

79

between Lloyd and me.

Upstairs, Lily is already helping to sort out Stella's room ready for her arrival. With each child there is always a sense that 'we are going on an adventure.' I leave her choosing some toys from her own collection that might be suitable for a five-year-old.

I'm not sure that I don't have an unhealthy relationship with my airing cupboard. People have a tendency to look at me strangely when I say that I love it. But I find comfort and deep satisfaction when I open the door to see the shelves of slatted wood piled high with neatly folded bedding and towels. As always, I indulge myself by taking a minute to look along the organised, colourful bedding, and brush my hand against the folds on each neat pile. This evening I take longer than usual, inhaling the mixed aroma of fabric conditioner and bars of lavender-scented soaps that are tucked away in the corners. I enjoy looking at the organisation of sleeping bags stowed in a regimented line on the floor, always laundered and fresh, ready for sleepovers at a moment's notice, camping and school residential trips.

In a world of chaos, and in a household that is regularly being upended by welcoming in the owners of damaged little lives, this cupboard is the place I go to when I need to remind myself that my world is, and will be, all right. I carefully edge a colourful patterned duvet set away from the pile. There is some pink in it, but not too much; I would never presume a little girl wants pink, especially not after living with Lily for the last few years. I find the matching pillowcases and carry them into the spare room that will now become Stella's room.

Lily helps me to make up the bed. The sheet and duvet are a little faded now, but it's one that Lily herself liked when she first came here. She smooths the pillow edges down carefully with her fingertips, and places a cushion in the middle, putting the finishing touches to the arrangement. It is a thoughtful act, and I know that she is remembering her own arrival here.

'Do you think she'll be hungry?' I ask, rhetorically, thinking about embarking on cooking the third dinner of the evening. Gleaning from the few notes in the referral that were read to me over the phone, Stella sounds thin. When I was in care myself, I went through stages of being starved or denied food as punishment, and my abusive adopted mother had an obsession with size. She liked small things. She was small, tiny actually, herself; and she liked small things: babies, miniature-sized packets of food, even small fruits. I was made from a different DNA and was as tall as she was by the time I was eight years old. My Amazonian build contrasted with her delicate frame, and she became obsessed with my big bones and feet. Her strategy to make me more like her was to repeatedly deny me nourishment, and she also saw the distribution of food as a way of having control over us children.

As a result of this early conditioning I always have too

much food in the house, as Lloyd is only too aware. Last Christmas I was carefully counting out equal measures of sweets into the children's sweetie bowls. Unknown to me, he was watching from behind the door. I was mindful to make each bowl look like they were equal portions while dealing with sweets of different shapes and sizes. I finished off with five Maltesers placed carefully across the top. Just as I was about to tidy away the bags Lloyd leaned in from behind the door and took my hand. He turned it over and in the cup of my hand were three little chocolate covered balls.

'It never leaves you,' he whispered.

So, hearing that any child is thin or malnourished triggers my concern and my own memory of the pain of hunger. I mentally scroll through the several options that I could soon have ready for Stella (knowing that I have chicken nuggets and chips in the freezer as a failsafe back up, because I've never met a child coming into care who doesn't like those).

Lily interrupts my thoughts to answer my question. 'Yes, she'll probably be hungry.' She shoots me a defiant look. 'But *not for vegetables.*'

She twirls around out of the room, a gesture that tells me she believes she has now conclusively won our earlier argument.

Downstairs, the boys are equally ready to be welcoming. My sons never cease to amaze and fascinate me. I always hope that being in a fostering family is a good thing for them. We have looked after some children who I have regretted taking in in the past, not because of the children themselves, but because we had no idea that their trauma would impact so much on our birth children. When Vincent was younger he would occasionally say that he hated fostering. In the hectic blur of blending families they can be pushed to the back of the queue, and, if we are not careful, their needs can slip to the bottom of the pile when the priority becomes dealing with a demanding foster child who is commandeering all your attention – not to mention the queue of all the professionals surrounding that child that also make incredible demands on your time.

Once Vincent wrote in his annual feedback form (even a primary school child, as he was then, does not escape completing a feedback form) that he didn't 'like' foster children very much. Our supervising social worker at the time made us get the children to complete a feedback form straight after a placement broke down. In this case a child had self-harmed in front of our children and Vincent, un-surprisingly, was confused and upset by the whole incident.

Even though we had repeatedly reported concerns to the team no intervention was made; but because Vincent wrote that he didn't like foster children, we were suspended from fostering for six months as a family. Sometimes I wonder what world some social workers live in. Vincent is much more understanding these days, but we still take care about seeking the opinions of both boys and ensuring that they aren't sidelined from the process. They are used to this by now, and news of Stella's arrival doesn't do much to interrupt the evening's digital gaming entertainment – except that they pop outside to the garden 'to get something for Stella.' So, within a short space of time, we are ready. Or at least as ready as we ever could be for what is about to happen.

Placement meetings are long and boring for the child, but Stella isn't here yet. I sit at the kitchen table with Dave, our supervising social worker, who we've been working with for the last few months. Lloyd is becoming twitchy, as we have already waited half an hour, which will throw his timings out for a call with another client. Because I am an author and artist I rarely have scheduled business meetings, but Lloyd is a graphic designer and has clients across the world working in different time zones needing to talk through jobs. Sometimes we wonder if social workers realise that there is a world outside children's social care, that although we are foster carers we might have other commitments as well as the children. But right now, Stella is the most important person in our world, so I make what I hope is soothing eye contact with him, and we wait.

We continue making small talk until the doorbell eventually goes. I try not to jump up in front of Dave. He is one of those social workers who gives the impression that he is quietly judging you because he writes everything down, which, while useful, can also be disconcerting. As an ex-looked-after-child who has spent many hours reading my own files, I can confidently state that anyone outside of this process is likely to be amazed at exactly what is recorded. My jumping up could be interpreted in various ways: as 'Louise is overexcited' or 'Louise is very animated' or even, 'Louise is anxious.' I have learned that it's best to play Mrs Average Emotion in front of social workers, though it is often difficult to gauge what 'average' might actually consist of when dealing with marginalised children. Lloyd gets up too. His face, I am pleased to see, has shifted from bored and frustrated to kind and warm. He is an ideal man for fostering, given that he cares very much about how children feel.

I open the door, only glancing at the social worker who accompanies the little girl. Lloyd swiftly takes care of her and leads her and Stella's small bag along the hall, which looks slightly less cluttered now that the boys have hung their school things up in honour of a new arrival.

This leaves Stella and me together in the hallway. Stella is just like a tiny bird. This is my first impression of her. A quiet little sparrow of a girl. Her face is hiding under wispy light-brown hair, but she stares through the wisps and up at me through goggle eyes.

I can tell that during emergency care she has been given some clothes from the carer's box. I have seen these outfits before. The carer sensibly buys job-lots of basic clothes when the sales are on. She has to have something for just about any age or size that comes through her door. As do we. So it seems that Stella may not have arrived with very much in the way of clothing. Not unusual.

I quickly dip my head towards Stella. I don't want her to know that I am appraising her, just as I am sure that she is appraising me. I always resist bending down to meet the eye-level of a new child, in spite of what the books might say. I think it's not appropriate for a traumatised child, who might be going through their own sort of hell, to feel overwhelmed by an adult's intrusive presence. I have learned to try to keep a polite distance to help them feel safe. I welcome her and introduce myself, but she doesn't respond – just looks at me with wide eyes.

Our dogs are a great leveller. I chat away about them, and our cat Pablo Picasso, who will be along later to say hello. Stella listens intently, as though she is hanging on to every word that I say, but doesn't join in the conversation. I ask her a question directly.

'Do you like dogs, Stella?'

Her face breaks into a broad smile and she whispers, 'Yes.'

That is the first word that she has said out loud so far, and it seems to be as good as an invitation, so I let them through to meet her. The hallway is instantly transformed into waves of wagging fur and delighted child. Both dogs are Chihuahua-Jack Russell crosses with the rather lovely breed name of Jackawowas. Douglas seems to have more of the Chihuahua temperament. Chihuahuas seem to love children and are the best 'meeters and greeters' a child could have: true to form, Douglas seems genuinely excited to see Stella, and she makes a big fuss of him back. Dotty is definitely more Jack Russell and, if you are an adult and not on the level, Dotty will tell you in no uncertain terms exactly what she thinks. I have had to put her in her little cage a few times when some social workers or their managers have visited us in the past; but she, too, takes well to Stella – and Stella to her. It gives us all something to connect with in the awkward first few minutes of arrival. Soon Stella is rolling around on the floor with both dogs as though she has known them all her life. It makes quite a picture.

'Ooh, you have made some friends there. Those dogs certainly seem to like you!' I say.

Stella seems pleased, and beams back at me: a winning gesture that radiates through her whole face.

I don't want to ask her if she has had a dog, in the past – I am acutely conscious of not wanting to reference anything that might make her homesick or sad; she needs to look forwards rather than backwards right now. Her ease around Douglas and Dotty certainly suggests familiarity, and that she might previously have had a dog as a family pet.

'You can help me take them for a walk, tomorrow, if you like?'

A little nod, still smiling. The ice is well and truly broken. It's going to be ok, I think.

When the social workers have gone, forms have been filled, files have been exchanged, and their stultifying presence has well and truly left the house, the children, who have been itching to meet Stella properly, make their own welcome gestures. The boys, usually preoccupied with gaming, Nerf guns and going down the park on their bikes have, unbeknownst to me when they went outside earlier, picked a bunch of flowers from the garden to present them to Stella. They are tied with a little ribbon.

She lights up again at this universal symbolic gesture of welcome. It is a tiny thing to do, but the value of such an act can never be underestimated. She holds the little bouquet in her delicate little hands and sniffs the blooms; it is quite adorable to watch. Lily looks at Stella and, with such kindness and the knowing that can only come from being in that position herself, asks Stella if she would like to come and meet her teddies. Stella nods and goes with her, holding onto her hand, and I notice that she is still clutching the flowers in her other fist.

Chapter 2

It is late into the night. The rest of the household is long settled, and I am relieved that Stella seemed to fall asleep quite easily, with a bedtime story read to her by Lily, who was a similar age when she came to us and may remember her first, unsettled nights.

I sit and pour through Stella's scant paperwork trying to construct a decent narrative, to get a sense of who Stella is, where she has come from, how her story has begun, and what has led her here to us. I am also alert to any noise from Stella's room, listening out in case she wakes up, has a nightmare, or is upset or disoriented in her new surroundings. The first night somewhere new is always difficult. Especially so when you are in a stranger's house and have nothing familiar around you. I am also conscious of the flip side: we have a little person in our house that we know next to nothing about, other than that she seems to like the dogs – and the flowers – and if she is going to settle properly then we need to find out everything we can to help make her feel as welcome as possible. Our bed is covered in a rustling patchwork quilt of her files and documents: the paperwork that has loosely stitched a life together. There isn't much of it, and there are holes and dropped stitches everywhere I look.

It's hard, and frustrating, to be this much in the dark when you take someone into your home. I always try to get a good picture of a child's background to understand what has happened to them along the way. If they have ended up in this kind of emergency placement then there is going to be a complex, probably traumatic history. Obviously, a child does not have a camera tied to their head, so I can never truly 'see', but having a decent backdrop of information can be very advantageous when helping them to deal with their trauma.

I get my detective hat on and begin to piece together what I can. Dates are missing on some entries, and there are a mixture of handwritten and typed pages. Much of the documentation seems to have come from teachers at Stella's primary school.

As far as I can work out, Stella was originally living with her mum, Shannon, who still lives locally in a nearby city according to the paperwork. I see that this area is now out of bounds to us while Stella is in placement; that doesn't present a particular problem, it's not somewhere we go to regularly, and I don't know anyone who lives there, so I can just make sure that we avoid the place.

For some unexplained reason, this arrangement with Shannon broke down quite quickly, within a matter of weeks. There is no note to suggest why, which is frustrating. Why does it remain unexplained? Even to know that much would be useful. Shannon was a teenage mum, so perhaps that was a contributing factor. From then on, it seems that Stella was in a series of 'kinship' placements with members of her father's family. I wonder where he was then and how Stella ended up with his family rather than her mother's. I also can't help but wonder if they were official, or if little Stella was passed off-handedly from one family member to the next. It looks like a woman called Cath, who must be Stella's grandmother, has been through something called the 'Form F' process of scrutiny to obtain a small allowance for Stella's care. I make a note to ask Debbie, Stella's social worker, for more detail. There aren't just a few dropped stitches here; there seem to be whole patches missing in the trail of paperwork that prevent me from establishing any kind of coherent story, other than that Stella seems to have moved around an awful lot in a very short space of time. But I am not surprised. In my experience, this pattern is all too common. Records and communication are always fragile in a fragmented system.

Next Stella seems to have spent some time back with her dad. I'm still not sure why she didn't go to him first, or why he wasn't there at the start. Perhaps he and the mother had already split up before Stella was born? I can't see from the file what has happened to him or anything very much about what he was like as a dad. There is just so little information to go on.

The trail picks up again when Stella returns to live with her mum in the middle of last year, having been apart from her for the best part of four years. There are enthusiastic notes from the social worker about how well Shannon is doing in her parenting sessions. *Not that well*, I think, given where she has ended up just a few months later. Those jolly updates don't seem to last very long. I wonder if this other social worker was being falsely jovial and upbeat – it's always a risk when you are trying to read between the lines in these documents, as they have multiple audiences. Perhaps the social worker was simply trying to be positive and optimistic, or maybe they had genuine reason to believe that things were going well.

I glean most of the information from the school's entries in the file. I can see that it was the school that was quite influential with the removal of Stella from her mother; there is a headteacher who has made repeated calls and reports of her concerns over absence and neglect. Some of her comments remain on the file directly:

Class teacher raised a concern during Stella's first PE lesson. Stella stripped off completely, folded her clothes into a neat pile and then stood entirely naked, for all to see.

Strange, I suppose, but maybe not unheard of in a four-year-old who doesn't understand about the etiquette of getting changed for PE. It doesn't sound too bad – but something has struck the teacher as odd.

Further bruises noticed on upper arms as Stella got changed for PE lesson.

Ah, ok. Some physical concerns, then. The school seem to have pursued it very doggedly, though. There is a suggestion of substance abuse on the part of the mother, Shannon, but the exact nature of concern in relation to Stella's safety is unspecified. There is nothing about poor behaviour; so often with children in care a lack of understanding from the adults around deems them troublemakers, but Stella, on paper, appears to be very placid and easygoing, just as she seemed to be this evening.

The rest of the file is just made up of the details about going into the emergency placement. Sometimes if the police have been involved there are copies of police reports, but there is nothing like that here. I make another note to ask Debbie for more detail. There is nothing much here to cause me real alarm, but the giant gaps make me uneasy. It is clear that there is something I am not being told. There must be more to Stella's story, or she wouldn't have ended up here with us.

I put the paperwork away, perplexed, and make a final check on Stella, remembering to put on my dressing gown. Dressing gowns: Don't get me started on these obligatory items. We have to wear dressing gowns around the house, just in case the children that we foster see that we have actual bodies. It is a warm night and it is totally unnecessary from that point of view, but I do what I am told. Most of the time.

I tiptoe across the hall and push open her door gently. She is fast asleep, her breathing is regular, and there is a little beatific smile on her face. She really is like a fairy child, so slight and her skin has an almost translucent appearance. I tilt the shade of her nightlight down a little further so that it dims the shaft of light that is cast across her face. I am yet to meet a young child who likes sleeping in total darkness, especially when there may be a history of trauma, but Stella seemed not really to mind at all one way or the other. It was almost as if she agreed to it to keep me happy. She didn't make any kind of fuss at bedtime, though I know how difficult a time of day that is for children – whether they are in care or not. There was a whispered 'goodnight' back to me when I tucked her in, but it was one of very few words she said all evening. If I think back, I can count them on one hand. That in itself isn't unusual for a shy child in an unfamiliar environment.

But, now that I stop and think about it, she is very, very quiet. She smiles plenty, but I'm not sure that I have really heard her speak out loud; she seems to mouth answers on her breath rather than disturb the air around her. She is so very keen to please, but in a gentle, passive way: an almost imperceptible nod with a compliant shrug has been her preferred response to every question so far.

Still, she looks at peace. I watch for a moment, savouring the beautiful tranquility of a sleeping child. Her brow seems to pucker up momentarily as though a dark thought has planted itself there, and I wonder again about the chain of events that have led her to be in this house on this night.

It is a puzzle and a mystery that her file has done little to answer. I can't help but wonder some more about this little stranger sleeping in our house. And consider how it is that she has managed to charm us all on her first evening with us by saying so little. She didn't seem distressed at any point in the evening. She played happily with Lily, who definitely did most of the talking. She joined in with the game of teddy bears' picnic when Lily whisked her off to meet the teddies (which mostly seemed to involve setting up toys around a tablecloth but not doing anything very much with them). All the while she seemed to be engaged, and quite content to be directed by Lily.

Even when she chose her sandwich snack, she did it by pointing at the cheese rather than the ham, and accepted it with a little bob of thanks – but no actual words. It didn't seem rude: the opposite, in fact. It was more like a grateful, humble curtsey.

And, through all that calm, she has us noisy Allens enraptured.

I watch some more. I can't help myself. But she looks so fragile that I feel incensed that someone has physically abused and neglected an innocent little girl. I wait until the sleeping frown has passed and then move across to pull the duvet up where it has slipped a little. I notice something in her fist. It is the blooms from earlier, which the boys gave to her. She is still clutching on to them for dear life. I smile. I manage to prise them from her hand without waking her and find a little vase to put them in, placing it on the bedside table right next to her so that it is the first thing she will see when she wakes up in the morning.

The next day dawns bright and clear. I am up early. When I check on Stella she appears to be still sleeping soundly. Good news. I begin the day full of optimism and determined to make it a pleasant one for our new house guest.

A little while later, Lily is holding Stella's hand as they walk down the stairs together for breakfast. They look very sweet: the older child leading the younger one. At times like this I remember exactly why we foster and I am so proud of Lily – who will argue that day is night and question every single thing we say – and everything she has already become. When I see her act in such a kind and caring way, I know that she will be alright: she is already turning into the powerful woman and force for good that I know she will one day grow into.

For Stella's first full day in the Allen household we take things very slowly, softly and gently. Our family's collective desire to support Stella is inspirational. I watch my sons show her where things are, explain routines and carefully detail how our household works. They do it all with patience and with kindness. It is a delight to see how they step up instantly to roles of protectors and teachers, helping Stella to balance on a scooter in the garden, getting things down for her in the kitchen that are just out of reach of her tiny fingers, showing her the rules of a simple card game. Stella nods in understanding at everything she is told, and tries each thing out, but says very little, preferring to communicate with polite nods and gentle little smiles. The less she says, the more that the other family members compensate and fill the air with talk, trying hard to make her feel at home. Recognising her fragility, the boys have even put away the Nerf guns for now. And Jackson has completely retuned his usually 'colourful' language. I'm impressed. I doubt that it will last long, but I will savour it while it does.

Lily is caught by the same need to protect little Stella. One of her first actions is to give her a strawberry shampoo and head-massage. Afterwards, she patiently coaches Stella about being a foster child, giving tips on how to fit in, explaining what the household is like.

'You'll like it here. I know that it feels strange at first. You'll get used to it.'

It is as if Lily has been doing this all her life. In many ways she has, having been in foster care for over half her life and with two other carers before she came here. I watch Stella's face, pale and interested. It holds so much good and kindness, so much trust.

So far, so good.

Sometimes you meet a child who brings out the very best in others. Stella has sprinkled her magic fairy dust over us all in the space of a single day. It makes the knowledge that she has been so neglected that she had to be removed from her parents even harder to stomach. Stella moves around our home and our hearts like a piece of scented paper. It's not an exaggeration: her aroma since Lily gave her the strawberry shampoo is glorious; her smell wafts round her like a magical cloud. Her movements are those of a little bird. Sometimes she shakes and sometimes she is still, but she is always alert, always watching. Though she is polite, affectionate, warm and open, she doesn't ever quite seem to relax, I notice. Those wide eyes are ever-attentive.

Lloyd is also more struck than he usually is at a new arrival. Stella's presence is powerful. He fusses over lunch, making sure that the snacky finger foods are exactly the right temperature, not too hot or cold. He suddenly seems to have acquired the temperament and attention to detail of a *Masterchef* contestant. He agonises over the buffet-style offerings, making sure that there is nothing on the plate that may put Stella off from trying out more food. I know that he is balancing this with seeing a little girl, thin and under-nourished in so many ways, that he is desperate to feed.

Stella seems to love fruit, especially the green grapes. After lunch I wash some more and leave them out on the kitchen table, making sure that the bowl is positioned close to the edge so that Stella can reach them without asking. I reassure her several times that she has permission to eat as much fruit as she desires, and am pleased to see that over the afternoon the grapes gradually disappear. Whenever they get low, I top them up again. Stella is probably not nearly as preoccupied about this as I am, but it satisfies my own need to know that children can help themselves as their appetites dictate, as opposed to my own experience of living in a home where the food was locked away from me and traps were set to see if I had taken any. My finger was always a surreptitious dipper into sugar bowls and jars if ever I had the chance. I see my children, who have always had access to food, be amongst it without being dominated by it – as I always am. This is also what I want to see for young Stella. Again, she seems to be taking everything in her stride.

In the afternoon we take a little walk as a family with the dogs. Stella asks if she can hold Douglas' lead. I know she would like to hold it by herself, but Douglas pulls like hell on the lead, sometimes enough to make himself cough. He is always in a hurry on the way to the park, and simultaneously busying himself with the important process of checking where his fellow dog friends have already weed earlier in the day. He is also liable to try and eat something disgusting en route, while also managing his other target of getting to the park as quickly as possible. Generally he is quite chilled on the return walk, so I suggest that she might be able to do that on the way home, and offer her Dotty instead. Dotty, though bolder at home, walks a little like a horse competing at the Olympic dressage with an elevated trot displaying her four white sock feet to best advantage. She is very particular about where she treads, and hates the wet. Sometimes I think she has a little internal dog-monologue that goes along the lines of, 'my hair, my nails, oh my!'

Today it's sunny, so no danger of paws in puddles, and it's nice to have a breath of fresh air. While we are out I notice a strange thing: that strangers, too, fix their gaze on Stella and seem as transfixed as we all are. She definitely possesses a quality that is a little magical; there is something inexplicable about her that draws the eye. As an ex-abused child and experienced foster carer this worries me as much as it fascinates me. I don't want to think of predators moving towards her. I hold her hand a little tighter whenever we cross a road. I feel protective in a way that I haven't done for years, not since the boys were small.

We let the dogs off as soon as we have crossed the road and got to the main path to the park. Doug is much calmer off the lead than on, though he always barks at Collies and Springer Spaniels. He was chased by a collection of working dogs as a puppy – and consequently expresses his opinion every time we see either breed. As soon as we reach the park, Dotty goes straight about her business. I bend down to pick up Dotty's little doings, using the thin black plastic bag as a glove. Stella watches closely as I tie the bag and place it in the red bin, affectionately known as the 'dog bog'. Stella frowns and seems surprised at my behaviour. Perhaps I was wrong about her having had a dog in the past. Her shyness doesn't seem to allow her to ask questions easily so I fill the gaps.

'It's funny, isn't it? It's never a nice job, but it has to be done. We musn't leave any of her poop behind. It wouldn't be nice if anyone else stepped in it. It's very important for dog owners to be responsible for their pets.'

It wouldn't be nice if I got a hefty fine, either, but I don't mention that.

Doug always does his doo in the same spot. Stella reaches him before I do, and appears fascinated by his poo. She stands and stares at it for a moment, and then, to my surprise, gets a stick and pokes at it as though it is a plaything.

I reach her and interrupt the game by performing the delightful poo-scooping action once more.

'Daddy just kicked it away.'

Still very quiet, and I can only make out her words because I am looking right into her face, so I am kind of lip-reading, but I think it may be the first whole sentence that she has said.

'Oh,' I say, slightly taken aback. 'Right. Well, we're not allowed to do that here in the park.'

On the way home Stella takes Douglas as promised, and then holds out her hands for Dotty's lead, too. She walks them proudly, leads held right up in the air. They get tangled up a little when they cross over, which makes her giggle, but she stops and patiently separates them each time. She is a caring child, I think, in spite of whatever has happened to her.

For the evening meal, as it is a Saturday evening, we all eat together. The boys come in one at a time and, once everyone is at the table, I ask Stella if she would like spaghetti.

She looks extremely confused. Her features light up with the first hint of panic. So far she has taken everything in without batting an eyelid.

I show her the spaghetti in the saucepan. It does nothing to alleviate her puzzlement. I smile reassuringly. After being brought up by a woman who controlled each child's portion of food according to what size she thought they *should* be, and knowing how unfair and wrong that was, I usually put the food on the table in a large dish so that the children can help themselves. Lily, I remember, struggled with this at first: she didn't understand how to share, or when to stop, but these days she is brilliant and takes only what she needs. It took her a long time, but I trust that children will be able self-regulate eventually when it comes to food. I can see that Stella definitely doesn't want to go first, and I suspect that this is less about self-regulating and much more about not knowing quite what to do at the table. But, as she has done all day, she watches carefully and follows the actions of the others. She is a sharp observer.

I am amused at how polite the rest of the family are: passing the cheese with multiple 'pleases' and 'thank yous'; filling up each other's glasses with water. I know it will not last long, but it's good to see that they do know how to do it properly from time to time. I have learnt that when they all ease back into more loose (I hesitate to say 'bad') manners, it's a sign of relaxing into themselves again – which is good too – but for this moment I can enjoy the heightened civilisation that Stella has brought to our home. I'm sorry that this weekend has to come to an end.

Caught up in my little reverie, I have taken my eyes from Stella for a moment. Now I see that she is really struggling with the spaghetti. This is definitely not a meal that she has encountered before. She was fine with sandwiches and sausage rolls and crisps at lunch. I am about to step in when Jackson, fulfilling his duty as the eldest, leans towards Stella and, just as we must have once done with him, asks:

'Would you like a little bit of help, there, Stella? Here, let me.'

Her relief is palpable as Jackson pulls her plate towards him and carefully cuts up the long threads of pasta into more manageable bite-size mouthfuls. I notice that he settles back into his seat a little higher, clearly feeling that bit more mature than he did five minutes earlier.

Stella seems to enjoy the sauce with lean mince and onions and garlic. She looks thoughtful as she clears her plate. Lily launches into an explanation about exactly why she has her tomato sauce without meat, and introduces Stella to another new concept: vegetarianism. Lily's speech is long and detailed and opinionated. I watch Stella try and take this in; those big, expressive eyes seem almost to reveal the synapses flashing alight inside her head as each new connection is made. She processes this wealth of information and confronts new concepts with a strange kind of acceptance. She is having to deal with a whole new set of people, conditions, relationships, routines, sensations

– all alongside embracing a new family. And new foods thrown into the mix for good measure. Her head must be reeling, but there is no resistance. It has clearly been a momentous day for her. Our brains are processing ideas every minute of every day so that minute by minute we become new people. It's as though I can see this process in action for Stella.

I resist the mischievous temptation to open up a debate with Lily about whether tomatoes are fruit or vegetable, just thankful that some vegetables are actually being consumed by her. I am so grateful to be part of this little snapshot of a domestic scene. And I am so happy that this little jar of fairy dust, Stella, has come into our lives. What a privilege to be able to offer this.

As ever, my thoughts are tempered with disbelief about the abuse that she must have suffered previously. I think back to the notes about bruising and neglect. Who are the people who do not see what we see here in this beautiful little girl; really, who are they? What makes them so hard and selfish? The rational part of me knows that it is drugs and addiction, it is not being in control, it is not being fully formed as healthy, rounded adults who are educated and aware enough to understand parenting and much more. Still, I feel angry at the world.

A petal on the floor catches my eye. Strange. I wonder where that has come from. Until I notice that under the table, on Stella's lap, is the little bunch of flowers from last night. She has taken them back from the vase and is still gripping on to them.

Chapter 3

July

It has been a while since a placement has gone this smoothly, especially an 'emergency' one in the way that Stella arrived with us. But, after just a few days, Stella seems to have settled into the rhythms of the household, and become a part of them – a part of us. She is always quiet, but also manages to be at the centre of everything. It is a peculiar but charming combination. It's not that she doesn't speak, more that she often chooses not to. She will happily answer a question, but rarely asks one. We still don't know much more about her, we simply feel her gentle presence. So it is difficult to truly judge, but Stella seems to have really embraced all of us and accepted our little foibles.

She has also been brilliant at trying all the new foods that we have introduced. She looks at some things – lasagne is one – as though they have arrived from outer space, and I guess that her diet must have been very limited thus far. Nevertheless, she is far more adventurous in her willingness to try things than Lily ever was – or is. It seems I just need to place something new on the table for Stella to really take to it immediately. She has no hang-ups about experimenting. This is something of a revelation, especially after Lily's recent behaviour in relation to food.

Stella is also generally very trusting, and open to all sorts of new experiences, not closed down and insular, as many children are when they arrive with us. The little bouquet of flowers (a mixture of sweet peas and violets) didn't last long, and Stella was sad when it came for the time to throw them away. I have an idea. I ask the boys to pick some more, which they willingly do, and then I show Stella how to press them in a little wooden flower press. She is not at all impatient for them to dry out, unlike Lily, who wants it all to happen in five minutes, and Stella is amazed by how they retain their colour if you press them freshly. She takes readily to painting and drawing and enjoys being in my studio with a pot of pens or paints, mimicking my patterns and illustrations with her childish hand, or at the kitchen table with some paper practising her letters. She is so willing to try things. I only have to suggest an activity or idea before she is nodding with a gentle eagerness. I wonder if this is borne of not having the opportunities before. She is seizing them now.

I have no qualms at all, therefore, when Lily approaches me to suggest a play-date with one of her best friends from school, Maria, in order to introduce her to Stella. It feels like another extension of the warmth and kindness Lily has shown to Stella since her arrival, and, though I get the impression that Lily wants to 'parade' her new foster-sibling to some extent as well, the intention seems to be to do so with pride and love.

Before agreeing, I check privately with Stella that she is also keen for this visit to be organised. When I mention Maria's name and ask Stella if she would like to meet Lily's friend, she nods eagerly and claps her hands together repeatedly, before launching into a chorus that appears to be made up entirely of Maria's name. Since she has said relatively little since she arrived, preferring to communicate with a simple nod or shake of the head, or to get by with the shortest response possible, I know this is a true endorsement.

'Okay, okay,' I say, laughing. 'I get the message!'

Lily, striking while the iron is red hot, straightaway asks if another friend of hers, Zoe, can come along for the play-date, too. I agree, remembering the old adage about three being a crowd and judging that adding a fourth is probably a good idea on this occasion. Before it escalates into the social occasion of the year, I put my foot down to any further friends. It's a play-date, not a party, and I'm anxious that we don't overwhelm little Stella in spite of her evident enthusiasm for the plan. Together we decide that a little afternoon tea for the girls will be just the thing. We can make some cupcakes and have some little sandwiches, and I can serve squash in a teapot for them. I ask Lily to think of other activities that they will all be able to enjoy together.

In the way of children planning something, this is already a done deal: Lily is quick to say, 'Dens, Mum. Obviously.'

I am not surprised. Ever since Lily arrived she has loved building dens, especially outdoors, and sometimes they become deeply complex with rooms and gardens and inter-connecting corridors and tunnels. When she builds a house I am amused to see how quickly Doug and Dotty 'settle in' too – and, if left abandoned for any length of time, Pablo Picasso, our big black cat, will always claim the best room in the den. I think there must be a feeling of security in building a den: creating your own space in a safe environment, but one that definitely doesn't belong to the adults, even if it mimics an adult world. Dens it is, then. Good idea. I make sure that there are rugs, blankets and sheets aplenty.

In preparation for the big day, a 'salon' is established in Lily's room. Lily takes charge of Stella's hair, brushing it into a ponytail to match her own. I'm not entirely sure about the finished look: is 'slightly wonky with a few clumps bent into shape across the head' quite the desired outcome? Probably not, but both girls seem enchanted by the result, so I am not going to interfere for once: this is their occasion and I'm enjoying the way that they are taking charge of all the details.

Little Stella also thrives on all the attention. It doesn't end with the hair-styling; next a generous coating of lip gloss is applied. Even then the makeover is not yet complete: Lily turns on her full Gok Wan and dresses Stella in a mauve sparkly top with a unicorn and rainbow on the front. I recognise it as a top I bought for Lily a while ago after she chose it and insisted dramatically that I buy it for her – then decided that, in fact, it was 'too much' for her, a step too far for a semi-tomboy. It suits Stella, though: she has embraced all things sparkly in her sartorial choices so far, and this ensemble in particular complements the otherworldly, ethereal force she seems to give off (and it's nice to feel that my money hasn't been wasted).

I think back to the notes I have been reading and re-reading at night. It was written in the referral that Stella was naked and filthy when she was found by the police at her dad's house. I hate this idea and can't get that terrible image out of my head. I look at her fresh, clean little body adorned in sparkles and colour – and feel a mixture of sadness and joy as I watch her dance with excitement when Lily tells her it's only two hours until the girls arrive. It's hard to explain 'time' to children. They busy themselves with other preparations. Lily suggests making some paper bunting to complete the tea party look, and that keeps them both busy for another little while. For foster children, two hours before an event might feel like two weeks – time inches forward for them both on this exciting day.

The boys make a tactical decision to disappear – the thought of being outnumbered by girls is evidently too much for them. They decide to hide in Jackson's room along with a large bag of sweets and the allure of the PlayStation.

'We'll be just fine, Mum. You carry on!'

I remind them to keep their language clean and not to go near the girls when they are playing.

'No chance of that happening,' says Jackson with a sour look on his face.

The sun is out. I clear the garden of any dog mess that may have been deposited since early this morning when I did my daily walk around the perimeter to check the plants and collect the mess. I go into the shed and pull out more of Lily's den materials. An old wooden clotheshorse that opens out into three sections will be useful for draping the blankets and old sheets over, and to serve as an internal wall of any den. A collection of old chairs and cushions will be good for rooms. We have saved a few tea chests and a couple of apple crates for exactly this sort of afternoon. Lily also brings down what seems like the entirety of her bedroom to add to the collection. I raise my eyebrows, and remind her that it will all need to be put back at the end of the play-date. I know that it will be me who ends up doing it, but I avoid making a real fuss: today is about Stella and her first opportunity to meet other girls who she can build friendships with. I tell myself that I don't mind the mess. It will be worth it.

I attempt to give the girls a sandwich for lunch. They are both so excited that they can't really eat. They flutter round the kitchen like little butterflies, unable to settle.

Lloyd has been in a few times with suggestions for use of even bigger cardboard boxes stowed in the garage. Show me the child that does not love a cardboard box to play in.

It's now only half an hour to go until Maria and Zoe will ring the doorbell. The atmosphere in the house reaches fever-pitch. Though I'm not really a football fan, I imagine it to be like Wembley before a cup final. These girls are going to be overwrought by the time the friends arrive. I wonder how we are all going to survive the afternoon. Perhaps this is all a bit much for Stella, so soon into her time with us, but as usual, she just seems to be getting on with it and taking it all in her stride.

The stage is set and I have done everything I can. Both Zoe's and Maria's mums are well briefed on the situation and know that behind this assembly lies a plan to widen Stella's social network. One of the greatest responsibilities for me as a foster carer is to show my children friendships – the key to the rest of their lives – that may be sustained long after they leave us. I am lucky to be surrounded by supportive parents who understand the complexity of our position and who don't see a foster child as a threat. Friendships are vital, alongside emotional intelligence. Often looked-after and ex-looked-after children have faux and inappropriate friendships that can dominate their lives even if they are damaging or dangerous. They might choose friends who are as high maintenance and abusive as the key people in their childhoods. I was in my twenties when I realised that my choice of friends was a continuation of the abuse and bullying I had experienced and that I ran round after people as I did with my foster mother, Barbara, trying to please – trying to be liked.

Finally, after what must feel for Stella and Lily like an interminable wait, the doorbell rings. In a second it is chaos. I shoo the barking, jumping dogs away into the kitchen (the girls are not the only ones excited about visitors) and leave them there temporarily as we prepare to usher everyone into the house.

Stella cannot speak, she is so full of excitement as she follows me to the hallway. I open the door to Zoe, who is holding out a bag of sweets. We welcome her in and her mum comes, too. I know that our friends, family and neighbours are always keen to catch a glimpse of a new ward. In some ways, it's a bit like having a new baby: everybody wants to meet them and see how we are coping. The girls stand in a huddle by the hall door. While I chat to Zoe's mum the door goes again. This sends the girls into such a state of heightened frenzy that I can't help but smile. Maria stands holding a shoebox of slime-making materials − glue and baking soda and brightly coloured tubes of food colouring − as her offering to the afternoon's entertainment. Sweets, dens and slime. These are lucky girls.

Now Lily cannot hold the excitement in. She squeals, which turns into a full-blown scream when she sees that as well as slime-stuffs there's also black food dye and black glitter in the box. Her happiness is entirely complete. Lily, I have noticed lately, has the beginnings of a lean towards the Gothic look. In fairness, I can't criticise: both Lloyd and I went to 'the dark side' when we were teenagers. I dyed my hair the colour of jet and crimped it like Siouxsie Sioux, but also had a penchant for wearing 50s dresses, sporting them two at a time, as well as an eclectic wardrobe of weird hippy clothes all of high colour and mostly from jumble sales. I was and still am spoken about as 'Louise with the hair and colour', while Lloyd favoured black and band T-shirts. Whatever Lily chooses to do, we will support her. (I have always had a thing against ear tunnel holes, but we are only at the stage of black slime so I'll get over myself and cross that bridge when it comes.)

The mums, as I do myself when dropping off a child for a play-date, seize on the opportunity of having at least one less child for a few hours and are gone in the space of a few minutes. I wave them off and close the front door. The girls have gone through into the kitchen and Dotty has finally stopped barking now she's realised that it's more children in the house. She is quite discerning. Children she loves; it's just social workers and a certain neighbour of ours that she has a problem with.

The sun is still shining, a perfectly beautiful summer afternoon. The girls talk a little about their plans for the next few hours and while they chat and create their play agenda I keep an ear out just in case Lily becomes too domineering. She is so strong-minded that she has a tendency to try to control everyone and everything. But all are in accord: they decide to build the den first, with a slime-making station inside, eating the sweets as they go. I fear for the blankets but keep my thoughts to myself. I open the kitchen windows wide in case I am needed, and this allows me to hear what they're doing.

Gradually the boys ease themselves away from the gaming and come down to see what's going on and, more importantly, if I have prepared the tea. They love a buffet – plenty of opportunity for chocolate fingers, crisps and small cakes to make away with. The tall cupcakes are the piece de resistance, and I don't want them touched until the girls have had first dibs. Vincent and Jackson stand outside the back door with mischief on their faces. I head them off and recommend the park. They shake their heads and refuse. I'm not proud. I offer them £3 each if they go back in and game. There is probably a special place in hell for mothers like me and I'm not going to win any parenting awards today, but I don't want anything to disrupt the girls' afternoon. They take the money and run off gleefully. It will stave them off for a while.

And the four of them really are having the most wonderful time. I stay close to the window while preparing a 'mainly' vegetarian feast. I am delighted that I can hear Stella giggling. She is really joining in and enjoying herself. I hear the older girls talk to her with so much patience and thoughtfulness, even though she says so little back. They are totally inclusive in spite of the age gap, and continually suggest things that she may like to do, prompting her to go first at each stage of the slime-making and play. It's great to see the way they are so deeply protective of her, and Lily is playing the proud elder sister role with admirable aplomb.

'That's it, Stella, just like that.'

'Careful there, you don't want to put too much in.'

Soon I call everyone to come and get their food. The boys fly down the stairs, fists grab one of the 'summer orange' plastic garden plates each and they are soon loaded up, but they have a sudden rush of manners and hang back to allow the girls to come through before they head on out to the seating area of the garden to sit and chat as they munch away.

I replenish the table with food (two boys seem to have had the effect of a small plague of locusts) and the girls tuck in. I watch Stella's little hands hover hesitantly over the bowls of various biscuits, raisins and grapes until she gains confidence from watching the older girls happily load up their plates. The girls take their food and sit back in the den, closely followed by a pair of attentive dogs fashioning their cutest faces. Dotty and Doug are experienced food wranglers from kind children.

While they are quiet with their mouths full, I set up the badminton net. I tie it to a tree and the wall where the previous owners have placed a plant hood just at the right height. Lily carefully explains the principles of the game and then they ignore them as they run, dash and scream at each other. Lily is deeply competitive while the other girls don't seem to be, but much laughter flows across the garden. I notice the boys watching the game while chatting like old men. I go and get

Lloyd's camera from his studio. This is an afternoon that needs a snap for the album. Happy memories are being made. Even Lloyd is drawn out of his studio, the deadlines now less pressing. Good. He is the far better photographer of the pair of us, so I'm pleased. He grabs a handful of crisps and comes out into the garden with me. We both inhale the atmosphere; we love these moments and it's great to share them.

Lloyd snaps away surreptitiously at the happy scenes. He likes to take candid shots. Our children are used to Lloyd recording their lives, and often, for foster children whose lives may have received erratic or little recognition and coverage, and where movement between homes means that photos of 'times before' are easily lost, there is great value in recording them engaging in fun activities or just 'being', especially if their early lives have been chaotic.

I call everyone together, channelling my inner director: today I want the group shot as well as the candid ones. The boys pretend to hate it and drag their feet around moaning as they are cajoled into position, but funnily enough, pop up grinning at the back. Vincent stands on his toes, determined to be taller than the girls. Maria is tall for her age so he steps away from her and runs to the other side of Jackson, who has been affectionately nick-named 'the Bear' for being the tallest and chunkiest in his class.

The girls manoeuvre little Stella, the star of today's show, into the front of the picture. Zoe slicks down Stella's threads of hair that have gradually escaped from Lily's handiwork with the ponytail. With much gesticulation I get them all into place. Lloyd has the camera ready.

'Say cheese,' I call out.

'Cheese,' chorus most of the assembled subjects in unison.

But, without warning, Stella throws herself onto the floor, pulls off her knickers, points her legs upwards in the air, and parts her legs to face the camera.

Shocked, Lloyd puts down his camera and looks at me. Though we have never seen anything like this before, we both know what it must mean. The other children are understandably confused and disperse back into different areas of the garden and the house – just anywhere that is away from the scene.

Blinking back tears, I walk over to Stella, who is still holding up her lower back with her hands, and pull her skirt across her thighs. I hold her hand and pick up her knickers, kneeling down so that I am right beside her. I look into her soft little face and pull her towards me. I try so hard not to cry, but I can't help it. My face crumples. In a single action an afternoon has been soured, but we have all just seen a startling depiction of how innocence has been totally violated, how Stella's right to be a child has been denied.

I lift her up and sit her gently down on the garden bench. She nestles in beside me, quiet and still. Try as I might, I really can't stop the tears from flowing down my face.

'Are you alright?' Stella asks, and the anxiety in her voice and the fear in her little face makes me feel even worse, especially as I think that this is the first question she has asked since she arrived. This is the wrong way round. I should be asking her that question. I know that I need to pull myself together.

Lloyd is doing a grand job of pretending to be interested in the plants, and can't find enough hyperbole as he admires the den and the slime factory with the girls. The boys are sitting looking downcast. Jackson is old enough to be able to guess at what that meant. I'll worry about that part later.

I sit with Stella, who clearly has no idea that she has done anything out of the ordinary, and try to arrange my thoughts. I take comfort in inhaling her strawberry-scented hair. We need normality, and we need it as quickly as possible. The mothering instinct overrides my horror and sadness. Food. I know there is a selection of mini ice-cream pots in the freezer. They were on offer at the supermarket last week.

'Who wants a Ben and Jerry's?' I call brightly.

Everyone shouts, 'Yay!' back at me, joining in the frantic grasp to regain a foothold into the ordinary.

Stella joins in with her own 'Yay,' mimicking the others, although I am pretty sure she has no idea about who or what Ben and Jerry might be, and is therefore oblivious to what she is cheering for.

I compose myself as I retrieve them from the kitchen, and there is much fuss about choosing flavours and opening the lids from the pots. We are all delighted by having something to do that will try to erase the snapshot moment.

But Lloyd and I keep looking at each other. We know that we must wait until all are in bed to have 'that' conversation. I know that I will have to write a report to Stella's social worker, as well as ours. I know that Stella will now have to go through the process of disclosure. It's hard and confusing for a child, and all I want to do is protect her.

The sun, somehow, is still shining. With some semblance of normality superficially reinstated, and as I have done many times since we began fostering, I mentally rehearse the awkward conversation I am going to have to have with the mums when they come to pick up. I sincerely hope they will allow their children to come again, but suspect that excuses may follow further invitations. I think about what words I can use to explain to Zoe and Maria's parents what has happened, knowing that I will try to make light of it. I need to have a conversation with Jackson – and a slightly different one with Vincent and Lily, who are just young enough for the sexualized nature of what Stella did to bypass them. There is part of me that wants to pretend that this just did not happen, but how can we ignore it? It will linger and ferment inside all of us. I want to rewind time and stop it from happening completely.

Of course, it's not about the ruining of a family photograph. It's horrible evidence of the ruining of a little life. For someone who really only seems to speak if she has to, and usually only when spoken to directly, Stella's actions really do speak louder than words.

Chapter 4

The dust settles once again in the Allen household.

It settles even though I think that it can't possibly. We work hard that evening and the next day to try and make sure that Stella feels none of the ripples of her reaction to 'say cheese.' Those two innocent words, that should conjure smiles, will never mean the same thing to me again. I'm not even sure that I will ever be able to say them again. They clearly don't represent an innocent command for Stella.

I am walking on a precarious ledge of uneven emotional places, but I try to distil the feelings until the main, overwhelming thing I have inside me is anger – anger at what must have happened to a five-year old girl to cause her to react in that way.

When we hear in an abstract way about the 'exploitation of children', it doesn't give any meaning to what that might actually represent in real life. It's a phrase that really does cover a multitude of sins and allows us to gloss over the reality beneath – the stuff that is just too difficult to consider.

Exploitation is really an attack – aggressive and violent in outcome. Exploitation means a betrayal of innocence. It is a sullying of that clean, fresh time of being a 'child'. Before dirt and rot cling to the mind and heart. There is no way to take that away again. It's a brutal sabotaging of security, a severing of trust in someone or something that will remain through the rest of a life. I know for certain that Stella has been the victim of some kind of sexual exploitation.

I fume and fume. To think that an ordinarily wholesome phrase such as 'say cheese' can be used as a way of controlling and enabling abuse is just too much for my head to cope with. The thought of what it means as a trigger to Stella is burning a hole through my soul. Her world must be more than warped. It is twisted back to front and upside down.

Lily wants to know if Stella is allowed out in the garden to play. I think she wants to recapture elements of yesterday and the fun that was had before the flash of a camera darkened our world. I help Lily and Stella get out the den-building materials from the shed once again. Lloyd is in his studio working on a brief about food mixers. I can hear his music and the live chat he is engaged in with a copywriter; it must be one he is close to and has known for years, or the music would be off. I have some work to do, too: my agent has asked me to submit a new synopsis for a book and I have 12 new illustrations for a greetings card company to start. But, instead of making some headway with that, I find myself leaning against the sink, watching the girls through the kitchen window.

Stella is so compliant, so amenable, so gentle. She and Lily work together well. Lily gives out the instructions and Stella instantly obliges. She sees me in the window. I wave and smile; she waves back and tells Lily that I am there, who is so used to me now that she just looks up and smiles and quickly gets back to work. The damage done yesterday is to us; the damage to Stella is from the past, but lives on continuously in the present. I want to do everything I can to make it right. I can't make it right, so instead I do what I always do to try and fix things – resort to food. I make a couple of drinks bottles up with water and take two Lion bars from the biscuit box. I take the snack out to the garden on a little tray and set it out for them on the garden bench near the den.

I call them over. Lily grabs hers and, as always, I remind her to say thank you.

'Manners cost nothing!'

'Thank you,' she trills, managing to be both sarcastic and appreciative at the same time. She just about gets away with it.

But the reaction from Stella is very different. She stares, transfixed, at the tray. There is fear – no horror – on her face.

'Stella? Stella? Are you alright?' I don't know what to think. I wonder if the sun has got to her, or if she has seen a spider. I check around the immediate vicinity, and into the space where she seems to be looking. All the children we have looked after seem to have been scared of spiders and bugs. I don't know why. But it doesn't seem to be that, and she can't seem to tell me. She never talks very much, but now she appears to be incapable of speech. She looks distressed, then vacant, then seems to crumple into herself, somehow.

Finally, she turns and flees to the end of the garden.

I look at Lily, who is busy munching away. Hasn't she noticed? Is it possible that Stella's actions are bypassing her, somehow? Perhaps it's the lure of her chocolate treat, inoculating her from Stella's unsettling behaviour?

By the time I get to her, Stella is crouched in the corner of the garden between two shrubs with the fence behind her, like a trapped animal. She is trembling and muttering to herself. I can't make out the words. Her wide eyes are unseeing of her immediate surroundings. Instead, she is in some other, horrible place in her past.

'Stella, are you ok?' I ask, knowing that she is not. 'Stella. Look at me. Can you hear me? Are you ok?'

'Yes,' she manages to respond eventually, her little voice quivering on the air, even though she too knows that she is not.

'What happened, Stella? Can you tell me? Did you see something? Did something scare you?'

She pauses for a moment and my world stands still, too. She nods, slowly, and I understand that this is both an acknowledgement and an end to the conversation. She can't, or won't, articulate what it is. After a moment I try to take her hand. At first she won't let me, but after some cajoling I manage to weave her fingers into mine and we walk back up the garden together.

'You're safe here, Stella,' I murmur. 'Whatever has happened in the past, you're safe here.'

We go past the garden seat, still hand in hand, when suddenly she pulls away from me, violently. What *is* going on? It's a really strange reaction. There's something about that seating area that is upsetting her. Did something awful happen to her on a bench? I change direction to circumvent that part of the garden – and I know that we are at a crossroads, here. I feel protective of Stella and I don't know what to do for the best. I can't protect her from something when I don't know what it is.

As an adult who was abused as a child myself, I know that she will probably spend much of her life trying to recall, to forget, to understand and to find answers – reasons – for whatever it is that has happened to her. Later in her life she will spend time trying to work out exactly what elements of what she has been through were 'abuse', to try and separate out and compartmentalise her experiences. Suffused within all that soul-searching will be the shame. Shame is something that I know only too well. Shame is like dirty water. It can't make you clean, however hard you scrub. It is dark and murky and stops you from seeing what is really beneath – unless you dare to probe the water and search for something. But then there is danger, because you never quite know what that will be.

When I was young there were public service adverts on TV. I vividly remember one about an old man asking a little child if he wanted to see his puppies or have some sweets. I remember how sinister it was. How far have the people who have abused this little girl taken the line of innocence and tied her little head in knots with it? I am experienced enough to know that a social worker, a police officer, a psychotherapist, or indeed any professional working alongside these vulnerable children can never know the full extent of the abuse and exploitation that someone like Stella has experienced.

My biggest fear for Stella is about the 'care' that will now be considered and planned for her, however well intentioned. There are long lists of children waiting to see therapists at CAMHS (Child and Adolescent Mental Health Services). It troubles me deeply that professionals repeatedly make the mistake of thinking that sticking a child in front of a trained adult is the answer that will somehow 'fix' the child. And it is at moments like this, when you are busy looking after a trauma-tised child, that you are repeatedly reminded that you are only the foster carer and that the 'professionals knows best'.

I have met enough children and teenagers in my role as a foster carer to know that on the whole these children are way too switched on to believe in the magic of a therapeutic process that is cheaply delivered in a package of six sessions. The children I have worked with struggle with the question-able sincerity of 'therapeutic-speak'. I have sat in waiting rooms, waiting for foster children to finish their 30-minute, or if they are lucky – or perhaps unlucky – hour-long sessions, only for them to hotfoot it out of the waiting room, get in the car and say, 'Twat, I hate her,' or a variation of that sentiment.

The question of who children choose to like and trust and who they don't fascinates me. I have a very good friend who is also an ex-traumatised child who grew-up with astonishing abuse, who always says therapists, physio-therapists and psychologists are 'just people', subject to the same fallacies as the rest of us. They have good days and bad days. They may not be terribly good at their work or they may not *always* be good at their work; they may be good at their work but simply having a bad day – or they may just be the wrong person for any given child. And yet, children are expected to sit in a room with them: someone who may be, even inadvertently, making them feel anxious or angry. Because they have been 'sent' there, we expect them to go through with it, without question, for their own good.

I have sat with children in my kitchen while rushed psychologists try to study and assess them in the space of a single hour. An hour in which frightened, untrusting children are able to give them very little to go on. As carers we are often given a multitude of tick boxes to complete in the same time and in the same room as the one in which the 'assessment' is taking place. It can feel more like a quiz than any sensitive understanding of an individual child's trauma, and I question its value for any of the parties concerned.

But it's always budgets versus best – and budgets usually win.

If an adult who is paying for a therapeutic service does not get along with the therapist, they can choose to go somewhere else; they are grown-up and they have that option. Children like Stella simply don't. And I just wish that she had more time to relax and settle into a new life here with us before the professionals open up her little mind with more things to navigate.

I have listened at great length to several friends talking about the experience of going to see a therapist. Reflecting on the encounters, and in some cases the 'ordeal', they have described how they felt being in that space. Sometimes I wonder if they were unconsciously putting themselves back into trauma. I also know that when I was a child I would have said *anything* that I thought the adult wanted to hear. The shame of what had happened to me was way too strong to be able to talk about in any meaningful way with a stranger. Too many terrible transactions of my heart and mind had already taken place for me to be frank and truthful. The emotional investment was too much. There are more ways of administering therapy than talking therapy: there is art, dance, drama, comedy and plenty more, but they aren't always offered. And so I really, really fear what lies ahead for Stella. And I can't do a single thing to stop it.

The only thing that I can do is to leave it a few more hours, before I start the process of reporting that will

trigger investigations and scrutiny for Stella. I am rumin-
ating all the while, thinking about how best to phrase what
has happened. If I am honest, how I can try to 'bury'
what has happened, somehow.

But this thing will not go away. I have to report that
something is troubling Stella. I have a solemn duty to
do this. And yet there is a part of me that feels that I
would rather keep quiet than know that I am about to
be responsible for more trauma. Because I know that the
resulting journey of disclosure will not always be easy, no
matter how good the intentions of those involved might
be. And worse: we are trying to look after vulnerable
children during an extended period of austerity, when
local authorities have ever-increasing fiscal demands and
even the possibility of therapy, in spite of my reservations
about the varying quality of it, is frequently considered
to be a luxury. Will Stella's fragile heart be knocked
from pillar to post waiting for outcomes of meetings and
decisions?

When I was in my forties I made a freedom of information request for my own files: I wanted to read about my
own journey from being fostered to adoption – and the other
events that happened in my life. I often think about what was
said and what wasn't: what story was chronicled through the
arrangement of a series of documents, authored by different
hands. I am still surprised at what the social workers felt was
and was not worth reporting, and the difference between

that paper narrative and my own horrific experience as I remembered it at the time. I am critical of what they didn't do, of the distance between me and the girl written about on those pieces of paper. To me that child seemed to shrink away from the centre of their thinking. In some cases it seemed to read that some of the professionals were more concerned about their own feelings surrounding my trauma. I hope that things have changed since then, but recent experiences (and I have had plenty of them) would suggest otherwise.

Can I subject Stella to this? I am not sure that I can be responsible for the prodding and probing of her porcelain heart and fragile mind.

But I too am a professional, and one who signed an agreement to do just that.

I sigh, audibly, as I boot up the laptop, as if trying to blow away the thoughts. And do what has to be done. I try to be as pragmatic, factual and unemotional as I can. My first draft is crisp and clean. But then I reflect that one day Stella may read this, just as I read my own notes years later. So I decide to add more detail about her, and about the day itself. What she was doing before the photograph and the call of 'say cheese'. What fun she was having. How well she has settled in. How excited she was about the plans for the day. How much effort she put into getting ready for the tea party. I describe the makeover, and organising the den materials and the laughter. How wonderful she *is*. I get quite carried away. It's kind of therapeutic for me, too.

And then I move on to recount this morning's bizarre development. What a great time Stella and Lily had been having together before I put snacks and drinks on the garden bench and something made her run away and cower at the end of the garden.

I am acutely conscious of my multiple audiences as I write: Debbie, Stella's social worker; Dave, our supervising social worker (who we really only see at the statutory monthly visit); but the shadow of a grown-up Stella falls across the screen as I try to write and I struggle to achieve the tone I want, a tone that is right for the person at the centre of this story.

Before I send the email with the various parties copied in, I feel the need to satisfy my own curiosity. I need to *know*. I return to the garden. I walk right around the bench in both directions. I contemplate it from all angles. I lift the heavy feet up on each side of the bench and check underneath. I sit on it. I look at it from the height that I guess Stella must have done. My scrutiny reveals nothing.

When I am done with the bench, I go back to the kitchen and pull out the drinks bottles I used and study them carefully, turning them round in my hands, searching for a clue. Lily has a purple one with a unicorn on, and the one I gave to Stella was clear with a built-in pink straw and glitter trapped in liquid in the wall of the bottle. I stare and stare, all the while twisting each of them around in my hands.

I gave the girls a particular kind of chocolate: Lion bars. So next I think about those – the packaging, the shape of them, exactly what happened as I brought them out. There was nothing wrong with the taste of them: Lily chomped hers down straight away and the boys shared Stella's later after she had gone to bed. I am so puzzled. There is nothing about the bench, the bottles or the chocolate that can explain Stella's reaction as far as I can tell. I just can't figure it out. It all just turns to dust in my mind and makes no sense at all.

I return to the laptop and hit 'send' on my long narrative, wondering what it is that I am missing, and resolving to find out, somehow.

And then I wonder whether, if there had not been an end to our garden, she would have just kept on running – away. It's unthinkable.

Chapter 5

I head into the studio to work on the series of illustrations. Florence and the Machine provide my soundtrack as I draft out the strange faces and animals that will be the paintings.

I turn the music up loud but it can't drown out my feelings. In fact, the lyrics feed them. Each creature I work on seems to end up with Stella's wide eyes. They stare out at me over and over again. I can't stay properly focused on what I'm doing. My mind is not entirely on the job. Not even partially on the job, really. I keep coming back to what could have happened to Stella in her short life.

I fear the worst.

I always do.

I know from my own childhood experiences of abuse that the worst is usually a good place to start and then I am neither surprised nor angry when the worst proves accurate. I am always sad. Sad that another child will spend the rest of their life learning to somehow live with the shame, while trying to fit into a world that is harsh and impatient.

While I was growing up, art was always my refuge and my solace: my safe place, somewhere that I saw as an area of calm in a sea of chaos – that was until I began earning my living from it. Now I have to be strong and remember that I love it while I work towards a deadline. I need to keep my own anxiety at bay. If I let the anxious monster in I will never like what I do or even finish it.

I hear the email ping on my laptop from the desk on the other side of my studio and leap towards it. I am grateful for the excuse to stop working. I need news, and I need answers.

I am hoping, firstly, to hear back from Stella's social worker, Debbie. I need to know much, much more about Stella's background, and I need to know exactly what is going to happen next as far as Stella is concerned.

I click on the Egress email. The Egress system is a secure, encrypted pathway that enables us to share documents and information safely online. The graphics on the system are currently showing blue to indicate that it has been updated. It takes a moment to go through the security codes and then I read Debbie's message:

I will arrange for a police visit.

The words jump out at me. Just what I didn't want to happen. Things are moving much more quickly than I expected. No chance for that little bit of extra time for Stella to settle in with us before the process begins.

There is more.

I have also arranged Contact with Stella's mum, Shannon, for Thursday.

What? *This* Thursday? Surely not. This throws me completely.

Can you make sure that you get her to the Family Centre near her school for 5pm?

I bridle a little bit at what, in my bad mood, I consider to be her bossy tone and try to remind myself that tone in emails is complex, while thinking: *Would it kill you to ask nicely?*

Contact, which I usually think of with a capital 'C' as Debbie has given it here, is the name for a supervised and regulated meeting between parent and child when the child is in care: a way of maintaining contact. When a child has been removed from their family, as Stella has, then Contact will generally take place, at least initially, on neutral ground like a family centre. Given that it has really only been a short time since Stella left Shannon, I am almost certain that this will be their first meeting since the separation. It is therefore a really big deal.

But I have a few reservations. Not only is this limited notice, it is really poor planning time-wise from my point of view. School finishes at 3.15pm. The family centre is close to where the school is, a significant distance away from where we live. In order to maintain some kind of stability, Stella has remained at the same primary school she began in, hence my very long school run for her each day, nearly three quarters of an hour each way, twice a day. I will be at school to pick

Stella up, then have time to drive home and virtually have to turn straight back around again in order to go back for 5pm. Why doesn't anyone consult us properly? Or at least think about the logistics of these things more carefully? I ask Lloyd if he is free to let the other children in and give them their dinner; luckily he is.

I slam the laptop closed, knowing that the illustrations will have to wait for another day. I am not going to get any more work done. Almost simultaneously, my mobile phone rings. I don't recognise the number. The caller introduces herself as WPC Watters and explains that she would like to interview Stella later today.

Christ. Can they not give her five minutes to calm down? It is now me who is struggling with tone: I can't make my voice conceal my concern – or annoyance.

But WPC Watters is patient and professional. She tells me that she completely understands my concerns – in fact she shares them. She explains gently that the interview will be kept short and quiet and low-key. Stella will not really be aware that it is an interview as such. She is just going to ask Stella a few questions and she will not be in uniform. It can take place in our kitchen, if that is what we would like. She promises that she will do everything she can to keep the whole thing as relaxed as possible. She asks me what time would fit in best with our family routine in the afternoon. She sounds kind. And I have a much greater sense of her being flexible, and trying to fit in with us instead of the other way round; the whole exchange seems far softer than the bossiness that I thought I detected in Debbie's email.

We agree that she will see us after the children have had their dinner and are settled for the evening.

I'm feeling a little bit happier. She sounds quite nice on the phone. Perhaps some good might actually come of it.

After dinner I shoo the others away to their rooms under strict instructions to complete homework before playing any games. They know I am edgy and preoccupied and shuffle off without much complaint. I even hear the rustle of actual books and paper, such is their inclination to please and appease. I have a few minutes to clear away the dinner debris and even manage a smile at Lily's empty plate. There were mushrooms, onions, tomatoes, courgettes and herbs in that sauce tonight and it went down without fuss, or even discussion. (They were chopped up very small, it's true; but it is a victory nevertheless.)

The doorbell rings a minute after 5.30pm and WPC Watters is as good as her word: not an epaulette in sight. Instead of dark serge she is dressed in an owl-patterned tunic over leggings and Dr Martin boots. It is not quite what I expected from a WPC, but the effect is totally unthreatening, especially when coupled with her broad smile and warm greeting.

I invite her in and she makes a joke of having to shout 'hello' over the sound of the kettle boiling so that the ice is broken immediately. Stella is seated at the kitchen table kneading slime, and our unlikely policewoman shows Stella her own squidgy keyring that is similarly tactile. I am impressed by her ability to relate to a child in this simple way within a matter of seconds. Worn into the woodwork of the kitchen table are some lighter patches in the grain, the result of where Lily and Stella have spent hours rolling and pulling and stretching their gooey lumps of slime. WPC Watters points out some of the shapes that they have made on the table.

'Can you see the tree with its branches? Look – and this heart? Right here?'

Stella nods that she can, and points to another mark, reluctant to talk, but keen to join in.

'Oh yes!' says the WPC. 'That looks like a face to me. Does it to you? There's the nose and that's definitely an eye. Do you think that sticky-out bit is an ear?'

Stella nods, while her face scans the rest of the table.

WPC Watters makes a big show of helping her search for more patterns in the wood. 'Is that a dinosaur I can see there?'

I begin to fear for the future of my table as now Stella changes the game and endeavours to roll the slime to create new patches in the wood. She is making her mark in so many ways.

We leave Stella engrossed in what is evidently therapeutic play. She seems quite happy and relaxed. I take the tea out into the garden so that we can talk without being overheard, and also show WPC Watters the garden bench and the surrounding area. We sit there to have our tea. I go through the whole story of the weekend's play-date and explain what happened when we said the fatal words at the polaroid moment. She encourages me to take my time over the telling, but is also keenly interested in the bench incident from the following day, and very supportive of the way that I had exhausted all possibilities in terms of looking for spiders, bugs, anything that might have prompted the peculiar reaction. She asks to see the water bottles and the chocolate. The chocolate has of course been eaten, but I do have the water bottles. She frowns.

'Maybe Stella had a similar one before and there was a 'deja vu' moment where they triggered a memory.'

It isn't an entirely convincing theory, but I like the way that WPC Watters is listening and thinking, and taking this seriously – and sharing theories about what might have happened. The sexualised behaviour at the photo moment is unquestionable, but we agree that some kind of traumatic memory has also been triggered at the bench/snack moment; it just isn't clear precisely what.

We return inside and I busy myself at the sink as attention turns gently and apparently naturally towards Stella.

WPC Watters' questions are skilfully probing while disguised as small talk. It really doesn't seem like an interview at all. There are no notebooks or paper or documents, but much is gleaned about Stella and her emotional responses to the moments at the weekend, and also in general. This is a true professional at work. There is no judgement in anything she says.

I know that in her line of work WPC Watters will have seen and heard first-hand plenty about what some adults can do to vulnerable children, and therefore understands about the complexity of response that can be elicited.

I have a friend who told me that her mum's boyfriend had sex with her when she was 11 years old. I said, simply, 'How did you feel?' without reacting with the shock and horror that such a revelation might ordinarily provoke in a listener. Encouraged perhaps by her knowledge of my own background on the receiving end of abuse, she looked me in the eye and told me that she enjoyed it, that she craved the physical pleasure. This isn't easy to hear, and does not sit well with the laws of our land and our understanding about child abuse, but I sense that WPC Watters understands this, too.

She admires the water bottle and asks Stella if she used to have one like this. Stella's head shakes, but she is unconcerned and it eliminates that avenue of possibility very clearly. Perhaps it was the act of placing the items on a bench? I don't know how she manages it, but the question gets asked without sounding odd.

Walking WPC Watters to the front door after what has, after all, been a pleasant visit – this woman is clearly a human being first and police officer second – she expresses her desire to learn more about Stella's father. When I reveal that Stella is also having contact with her mother this week for the first time in a while, she rolls her eyes, understanding the unfortunate timing. I promise to keep her updated. Stella was removed because her mother's care was considered inadequate and neglectful and because Stella was at risk. There is nothing on Stella's file about sexual abuse, but there is now a distinct possibility that this has happened at some point in the past. Her mother could be connected directly or indirectly with it. Given that these memories have been so recently triggered over the weekend, I am doubly concerned about the contact arrangement. Until we know more, it just seems bizarre. An extra, unnecessary layer of emotional turmoil for Stella to have to negotiate at a difficult time.

I walk back into the kitchen, my mind churning. The meeting with WPC Watters went totally smoothly, and Stella is in no way upset. But now comes the more difficult bit. I have to tell her that she is seeing her mum this week.

Before I do, I wonder again why Debbie, particularly, felt that this was a good idea – right at a time when aspects of her behaviour were clearly indicating trauma and possible sexual abuse and exploitation.

I think that I will ask the 'why' question outright. After all, why not? We work so much in the dark as foster carers. If I can't find the answers that are lurking in Stella's past, then perhaps I can at least find some that will inform the decisions being made on her behalf now – in the present.

I decide simply to give Debbie a ring. I say 'simply', but this is not as easy as it sounds. I find the politics around talking to social workers very confusing, even after all this time. Sometimes you need to go through the supervising social worker in order to reach them, but I am increasingly reluctant to be bound by bureaucracy. I dial the number. There is a long automated message: call this number if you're a parent or a child, call that one out of hours, press another button to report a concern. The list goes on. Eventually I get Debbie's voice mail. How can I attract her attention to get back to me? Social workers are very busy and there is a shortage of them in my area: every social worker I know is taking on more cases than they can reasonably cope with, and part of a social worker's survival strategy is to leave the less important calls and prioritise the emergencies. I say, very carefully, 'I need to talk to you about Stella. Can you call me back please,' but make sure that there is no questioning uplift on please. It is a statement and very matter of fact. I hang up knowing that I won't hear from Debbie until tomorrow at the earliest, if at all. But I resolve to try again in the morning, and to keep trying until I do get hold of her.

I return to the kitchen. The slime is being pushed back in its little pot.

Now to handle the idea of contact. I ask Stella very gently if she can remember the last time she saw her mummy. Suddenly, her elfin features are suffused with longing. Her whole face transforms in an instant and I can see the deep desire manifest itself in the 'o' shape that she makes with her mouth and the way her big eyes fill, suddenly.

As so often happens, I can equate this with my own childhood yearnings: I too remember desperately wishing and hoping that my birth mum was going to 'be fine' somehow, and turn into the maternal figure I dreamed of. I know only too well the astounding level of attachment children can have to people who let them down repeatedly.

Next I ask her if she would like to see her mum soon. She giggles and nods. I can't really argue with that. I explain a little about when and where the meeting will take place, trying to normalise something that is emotionally strange and challenging.

I hope, Shannon, that you are worth it, I think. I say a silent prayer for a woman I have never met. The historic records on file are so erratic that it's hard to gauge whether or not Shannon was kind to Stella, but usually a young child wants to see their parent regardless of what has happened in the past: it's only when they become a little older, perhaps 11 upwards, that children seem to figure it out. As foster carers we are told to support and encourage contact, but sometimes contact can be deeply harmful, and there is usually no way of knowing how it will turn out in advance. But in this instance, there is nothing I can do. We shall find out in due course and, if it becomes a positive experience where Shannon is sensible and Stella gains something from it, then I shall have no complaints.

She lifts her head up and focuses those large, plaintive eyes on me. 'When am I going to see Mummy?'

There is such a yearning desire in the way she says the words that my heart breaks a little. I explain that we will make the visit on Thursday afternoon, after school, so that there isn't too long to wait. It is only three more sleeps, and it is time for one of those, now.

Chapter 6

Over the next couple of days my mind is preoccupied with the contact visit. Lloyd and I keep trying not to discuss it directly, or even mention it to each other, but it hovers there in the background of all our conversations. When you have a child in your care, you inevitably step into their world: their lives and dreams. You cannot help but be protective and do all you can to keep them from pain and harm – especially a poppet like Stella.

Both of us have fallen for little Stella in a big way and I feel that inevitable tug when I think about her seeing her mum. I wonder what it might dredge up from her past. To Stella herself, I try and keep all discussion about the contact to a sensible level. I'm always calm and try to downplay her natural excitement – and natural anxiety – given the circumstances.

The afternoon before the visit is scheduled to take place, I ask Stella if she would like to make a card for her mum, or bake some cakes. She chooses the cakes. I am yet to meet a child who did not want to learn about and get stuck into baking: there is a magic in turning a bowl full of disparate ingredients into something so unlike their constituent parts. Since having children in my life, my cooking and baking skills are now so sharply honed that I hold multiple recipes and ingredient quantities in my head without any need to consult a cookbook.

We measure out and combine the ingredients for sponge, then spoon the mixture into the paper cases that Stella has chosen and carefully placed in the baking tray. Once they have cooked and cooled on the wire rack, we set about making butter icing for the tops, and choose some sweets to decorate and embellish them with. Stella is very proud of her achievement. Lloyd takes a photo, but he picks up the camera with a heavier heart, and is mindful not to ask her to say 'cheese', or indeed any of the other things that people say when they want a smile in a photo. I wince a little, too, but move my thoughts quickly back to the task in hand. We place Stella's cakes onto a sheet of baking paper and arrange them in an old 'Celebrations' sweet tin that we label, all ready for contact tomorrow.

In the morning our children crash about the house in their usual chaotic rhythms.

'Where are my socks?'

'Vincent took the last waffle!'

'Have you washed my PE kit?'

'Time's up, you've been in there ages!'

'Anyone seen the charger?'

'Mum! Is it swimming today?'

All the pandemonium of family life writ large in the few moments before departure. I watch Stella watching. As she observes the children's movements in the morning, she looks eager to be just like them, to possess the confidence and security they have to be able to move as they do. She doesn't yet take part in the general flap of the morning, but takes it all in. And she seems to love breakfast particularly, a meal that many children who come into care are not familiar with.

She is dressed in her yellow gingham school summer dress, ankle socks with quite a high frill of lace – her own selection – and her hair is brushed with a slightly different parting. She has placed some sparkly turquoise clips in the front of her hairline. I remember that Maria wore a similar look the other day for the play-date, and smile inwardly at the implied compliment to the older girl. I love watching Stella quietly and politely inch towards discovery of herself and her identity.

Stella is very proud of her new clean school uniform; her old one had the worn appearance of being dragged from the lost property box. She has new black strap shoes with a little perforated flower design across the top that she has not stopped touching since we brought them home from the shop. I know that lots of other girls have them at the school; it's a popular design this season. Most children just want to fit in when they are little. It's only once they have fitted in and feel secure and safe that they can maybe start stretching the uniform boundaries. I notice Vincent has folded the bottom of his sleeves under: he has started the little rebellions already and he hasn't reached the top of primary school yet. I dread to think what secondary school will bring in that regard.

The boys and Lily make their own way to school. Theirs is just a short walk away and there is always a snake of children heading in the same direction once they reach the main road. Stella clambers into the car with me for the longer drive to her school, a few villages away.

En route, Kiss FM is her station of choice as there is plenty to sing along to in the mornings. She sings shyly, from the bottom of her mouth. It's a strange action, a small step on the way to finding her real voice in the world. I look in the rear view mirror at her and smile as she clutches her new school rucksack (that is also covered in the ubiquitous sparkles) to her chest. I force myself not to refer to mum, and what is happening later. I know that she won't have forgotten – it is too important an event. But she has not spoken about it this morning, so I won't either.

I pull into the car park and let a cluster of parents and children walk by before opening the door. I'm aware that the other parents and other adults – teachers and teaching assistants – all know about Stella and her story, and are likely to know Stella's mother, too. When I first began fostering and dropped off and collected children I often felt like I was being judged, as though I had done something wrong in some way. It was a strange dynamic. These days I am much more assured. I know why I am here. I try not to give away more information than I need to: I am there for Stella, primarily. But even though we are surrounded by a sympathetic community, I sense that she is still a little hesitant in this environment. Stella is shy naturally, and probably feels like the 'odd one out' with her complicated background. Part of my role is to help her to see that she isn't that different. Many children are in care or living with relatives, there is no such thing as 'ordinary' family life, and the world generally is far removed from the idealistic advertisements we still see on television screens and billboards.

But I also appreciate that Stella is far too young to comprehend all of this. I would like to invite her friends round for tea, but we really live too far out of the area to make it terribly practical. Though there is a middle-class Range-Rover element, the school is in an area that has historic poverty. New industrial investment has brought new housing and well-paid and educated workers. It is quite a social mix, and I suspect that not everyone around here has a car for transport. In any case, it is just too far to ask people to travel for a play-date. I'm going to have to continue to think of inventive ways to provide a social life for her.

Stella steps out of the car, brushes down her skirt and reaches up to hold my hand. I melt. We walk along the pathway towards her classroom together. She has still not brought up this afternoon, so now I do remind her gently that she is seeing mum later, and as a treat I will take her to the Rose Gardens café not far from the school. From my point of view it's also a practical arrangement that means that instead of driving home and straight back in this direction, we can be much more relaxed about the whole thing. Afternoon tea will kill a bit of time and we can look around the shops, too. It will be a treat for both of us. Stella looks excited and, with the grace of a tiny angel, steps away from me and stands in line for the teacher to open the door.

After driving away from the school I follow the satnav to the family centre in order to get my bearings in a trial run for this afternoon. I need to feel calm and in control, not panicking because I can't find the place later: Stella must have nothing but a smooth glide to contact. I find it easily. There is plenty of parking. The building is just as I expect: brick-built with a porch at the front, security buzzers for access and a big logo in yellow above the door. It's like many of its counterparts, thrown up in the late 80s and early 90s when there was more funding around than there is these days. I stem that unhelpful line of thought and turn the car around.

With the route sorted I head home to catch up on my logs and illustrations. I telephone Debbie once again, but there is no answer. I would really like to talk to her, to understand *before* the contact visit takes place exactly what is going on with Shannon, and why the decision has been made for contact at this point given the weekend's disclosures and subsequent police visit. I remind myself that social workers are up against it, as a way of trying to curb my frustration. I wait for another couple of hours and call her again. I am greeted by the familiar, long, soul-destroying message and hang up once more. I wonder how many other foster carers give up trying to get in touch because of that message.

Time creeps on through the morning. Today I am happy with my illustrations. I become completely lost in my work and am able to put this afternoon's visit out of my head. I feel a release when I'm fully absorbed like this, which is one of the justifications I have for encouraging children who come into care to do art: it's such an important activity for all sorts of reasons. Although I am drawing animals for this commission, I find that a little yellow gingham pattern has begun to creep its way into the design. I know why that is.

When I leave at around two o'clock (earlier than usual to make sure that I can find a good place to park and get Stella to the Rose Gardens in plenty of time for her afternoon tea), Lloyd is up to his elbows in illustrations and instructions for one of his biggest clients, a maker of pharmaceutical machinery. He knows that I am worried, and tries to make me feel better by inviting me to laugh at the poor models in the frame – likely engineers dressed head to toe in protective white suits and blue masks. They look like the cast of *Silent Witness*. I know exactly what he is trying to do and I'm grateful to him for the moral support.

At the school gates Stella greets me with that glowing smile.

'How was school today?' I ask.

She inclines her head forward, a gesture that I have learned to interpret as 'yes, fine'. She still prefers not to speak too much if she can help it, though she is communicating all the time through looks and nods and little inclinations of her hands. She still seems relaxed, far calmer than I am, and not for the first time I wonder at the resilience and emotional maturity that young children can possess. As with almost everything, she seems to just be quietly taking it in her stride. It is me who is more bothered about the whole encounter.

I have brought some coloured pens and a colouring book to help pass the time in the cafe until contact, but first we wander around the few shops on the parade near the school. There are a few nice boutique shops but mainly it's charity shops that we find ourselves browsing in. I'm on edge, though. I'm not sure if Shannon lives near here, or if the venue was chosen for convenience to the school. I don't know why 5pm either – it still seems an odd time to me – but since I haven't been able to speak to anyone about it, I have no answers. I remind myself, somewhat ironically, that I'm only the foster carer. What do I need to know for? Ours is not to reason why.

We enter the Rose Garden. I don't know the place very well but it's perfect for us. The tables are covered in thick tablecloths patterned with giant roses. It is a warm, harmonious place, populated by a few elderly people eating meals and a few other children with their mums or dads doing what we are doing. Well, not *exactly* what we are doing. I don't expect many of them are preparing their charges for a potentially difficult meeting with an estranged parent, but you never know.

The clink of cutlery on crockery acts as percussion for the bubble of chatter, and the symphony is completed by the whirring cacophony of the coffee machine. Steam from frothing cups fills the air. Stella looks positively animated as I present her with the slightly stained paper menu. She can't read the words yet, but enjoys the 'adult' experience of being invited to choose from it. She sits with a perfectly straight back, and politely glances at the squiggles of black ink and all their promise. I have already seen her eyes drift towards the cakes under glass domes near the counter. I suggest we go and have a look. The cakes are set perfectly to the height of Stella's eye-level.

'Which one, then?' A difficult question, indeed!

Stella's finger slowly moves from one enticing dome to another. After much deliberation, she eventually settles on a layered coffee and walnut cake and a big glass of milkshake. As is her way, she points and looks up at me to make her choice. She is still shy and finding her voice.

I love special, one-to-one time with children, especially when a treat like this is involved. I think it reinforces the notion that they are worth doing something nice with. And it really is an absolute joy to be in Stella's company. She has such a strong sense of wanting to live her 'best life', always.

She is so observant of other people's behaviour, and trying to assimilate it into her own. I never have to explain what to do, even when we take her into what I think are new environments and situations. Her watchful nature means that a rule never has to be explained. And it's peaceful to be around the aura of serenity she exhibits. She is so different from other five-year-olds. She seems so much older, somehow.

I have left us plenty of time; more than enough, so that there is ample opportunity for all that sugar to be digested before we head over to the family centre. I needn't have worried. The whole lot is gone in about a minute. There is nothing wrong with her appetite. I am left with just a few crumbs on a plate – and a very contented little face in front of me. Stella is happy to colour in for a little while, as I watch the clock until precisely ten minutes to five, when we leave for the centre, just a few streets away.

Here we go. I feel an overwhelming sense of foreboding as I stand beneath that yellow logo, finger pressed to the buzzer. I check Stella's face for any last residue of cake as we wait. I really don't know what this afternoon will bring. I am desperately hoping that the contact worker is a good one. The contact worker has a complex role: they need to maintain a healthy, professional distance from proceedings, while simultaneously observing and recording everything that happens during a contact visit. They need those eyes in the backs of their heads that my teachers always claimed to have.

Every now and then you might be unlucky enough to get a loose cannon who doesn't fully understand the role or hasn't yet finished their training. I'm relieved to see that today it's a face I recognise, a woman of similar age to me named Rita. She worked with the family of another little girl we fostered, and her family, a few years ago, so we know each other reasonably well. She is the perfect balance of being lovely and welcoming but, like a hawk, she sees everything. Stella is in good hands.

I say goodbye, and return to the car to wait for the allotted hour of contact. Technically I could leave and return to the shops or the cafe, but I stay close by just in case there is a problem of some sort. It wouldn't be the first time: most parents value the time with their children, but I have seen some contacts used as a way of causing more trauma or passing on things like mobile phones, or some inappropriate information, and a child needs to be removed at speed.

To pass the time I call Lloyd, who is busy loading the dishwasher. In the background I can hear Jackson and Lily laughing; Vincent is already on his computer game.

'How did Stella seem when you picked her up?'

'Calm. Absolutely taking it all in her stride. Not like me,' I joke.

'Did you have a chance to get a look at the mother at all?'

'No. I deliberately got her there right on the button to try and avoid that. She remains an unknown quantity, I'm afraid.' I never really know how I feel about meeting the parents, so part of me is genuinely relieved not to have encountered her, though I am, of course, intrigued by what she might be like. I read my book and listen to the radio until it's five minutes to six – when I leave the car and press the buzzer once more. Stella and Rita are already standing together in the hall, waiting.

It is immediately apparent that all is not well. Stella's face is tear-stained and she is catching her breaths in giant shudders, the way that you do after a serious bout of sobbing.

Rita looks mortified. 'I just don't understand what happened,' she explains, shaking her head. 'They seemed to be absolutely fine. I didn't hear or see anything untoward. And then all of a sudden, totally out of the blue, Stella started crying and shaking. Honestly, I don't know what's caused this reaction.'

It is clear that something has disturbed Stella deeply. The catch in her throat and those muscular tremors are abating, but she has clearly been badly shaken up by something. Again. I take Stella's hand in mine. I just want to remove her from this place and take her home, which is what I do. I feel deeply troubled once more. I have seen children try to run or back away from contact as soon as a parent appeared, but not disintegrate part of the way through the visit. What on earth can have happened during the contact – and under Rita's infamous beady eye, too? It feels, somehow, like the garden bench incident… Something that should be innocent becomes filled with something horrific, unseen by everyone else, but terrifying for a five-year-old girl.

Chapter 7

This time it takes a long while to settle Stella down and get her to bed, but she does seem pleased to be back in her room. She is such a good girl and so clearly desperate to please that I really think she is trying hard to control her emotions as much for our benefit as for hers. She seems to have an innate desire not to upset anyone or cause trouble. Eventually she falls into an uneasy sleep.

We spend some time downstairs with the other children, supervising the finishing of homework (or in Jackson's case, the starting of the homework that is actually due in tomorrow). I busy myself tidying up the kitchen and, after Lloyd has finished his last overseas conference call, I pour us both a glass of wine and we sit down to watch a film, but I'm distracted and can't follow the plot properly and neither of us is able to really settle into it. We turn it off part way through. Lloyd senses my need to talk it through and try to make some sense of things. He's just as perplexed as I am. There is just no obvious explanation, however much

I go over it in my mind. I wish that there was a way I could have spoken to Rita at length, but my first instinct in the moment was just to get Stella out of that centre and away from whatever it was that had upset her. I check my phone. Rita is still in my contacts from before. It's too late now, but I will call her in the morning. I rack my brain trying to think of other things that I can do, but my options are limited. It is another troubled night for me, too.

But the sun still rises in the morning, and Stella seems more stable: quite happy to go back to school and for normality to resume. We go through the morning routine once again. As soon as I have seen Stella into her classroom, my fingers are reaching for the phone and scrolling for Rita's number.

'Morning Rita, it's Louise Allen here, Stella's carer.' My voice is as light and cheerful as I can make it.

'Ah, Louise, how are you? I thought I might hear back from you. I am actually just writing up my notes from yesterday for the portal now.'

Formalities out of the way, I become myself. 'Christ, Rita. You saw the state of Stella there at the end. And it took a good while to get her to calm down properly. What do you think could have happened? Did mum say something, or do something?'

'No, nothing. Honestly, nothing at all. Not as far as I could see. It was so strange. I've never known anything quite like that. It really came from nowhere.'

She goes on to tell me how Shannon was calm and played with Stella all the way through the visit, picking up toys and dolls from the collection at the centre for Stella to play with. Then they were looking at a book together and having a little snack and it was at that point that Stella's behaviour transformed and the tears suddenly burst forth from her. They were uncontrollable.

'Of course, I stepped in straight away and tried to comfort her, as did Shannon.'

I ask what exactly Shannon did to try and comfort her.

Rita thinks for a moment. 'She spoke kindly to her, very softly, very gently, and tried to hold her, but Stella pulled away and hid behind a chair.'

We are both quiet for a moment. I'm replaying the scene as it has been described to me, and I imagine that Rita is reliving it too, searching for any clue.

'Has she done anything like that before?' Rita asks.

Without going into too much detail, I explain that this is now the third time that Stella has had a peculiar reaction to a seemingly innocuous situation and I can't figure it out.

'Well, you and I both know that trauma is a funny thing. Perhaps she has triggers that make her feel insecure or anxious.'

'No sh**, Sherlock,' I want to say in reply, but resist because a) I like Rita a lot and think she does a good job and b) none of us knows quite what is going on here and, as the saying goes, sometimes a little bit of knowledge is a dangerous thing. Instead I thank her for her time, and ask her to call me back if she thinks of anything else later on that might help. I also know that I am going to fight more against future contact given how upset Stella has been by it.

I sit in my studio with my laptop to write my own log, but because I know how important this is, and how imperative it is that I create a good paper trail, I email my concerns to Debbie, and carbon copy Dave, too. I explain that I have tried several times to talk to Debbie and feel that, given what has happened, I need more information in order to understand the thinking behind introducing contact with Shannon at this stage. I also leave a message on Debbie's phone, and text her, just in case she misses my voice message. Then I print out my email along with the previous ones that I have sent and put the hard copies in a file.

Years as a foster carer has taught me that it needs to be belt and braces when it comes to records. If there is a problem, the Egress security system can lock you out and limit your access to data that you yourself have generated. We have been advised not to keep paper records, but given that I am only printing out my own words, and I want to keep track of exactly what is going on here under quite difficult circumstances, I feel justified. Seeing as I have a lockable cabinet, I can keep them safe. You just never know.

Once again, I hear nothing. I feel totally helpless. I pick up WPC Watters' card and study it. In the absence of any response from anyone else, I decide that she might be a good person to tell about the latest development in poor Stella's saga. Her phone goes straight to voicemail, too, so I send a short, explanatory email to her as well. It can't hurt.

I spend an hour in my studio drafting out number four of the 12 illustrations: they are more disturbing in appearance than I would like them to be, and than I imagine a greetings-card company is going for. I'm not happy with them.

My mobile goes: it's the WPC. I'm impressed by her efficiency, which is in stark contrast to Debbie's at the moment. She apologies for not answering earlier and explains that she was in a meeting. Again, her manner is so very human, and considerate. She makes me feel that I am not wasting my time: a novel experience indeed. I explain about the contact visit and hear myself punctuating the conversation regularly with versions of, 'I don't understand why they are insisting on having contact.' I'm beginning to sound like a stuck record, even to myself.

WPC Watters is very professional as she explains over and over that we can't all understand the thinking of social workers. They are in possession of information that we are not necessarily party to. She manages to sound as though she is siding with me without denouncing the individual and the system that I am being critical of. I am reminded of all the reasons why I felt that I really liked this woman when we first met; she handles everything so steadily. I'm heartened when she reveals that she too has been trying to get in touch with Stella's social worker, but disappointed that, like me, she has had no joy from Debbie. And, like me, she will keep on trying. At least there is someone other than me keeping a record of Stella's reactions to her mum and a garden bench. It's a fog I can't work through, that won't lift, but at least there is someone else stuck in it with me.

I go and sit in Lloyd's studio, seeking the reassurance of human contact. It's a very different experience from my light, bright, white room. His space is dark with panelled walls, more like a Victorian gentleman's smoking room. He likes it dim so that he can see the screens on his large Apple computers. He generally has two of these running at the same time, as well as his laptop. We are so different, and I marvel again at the variance in human nature, even between two people who married each other and live in the same house. I look at his screens and feel myself glaze over, but am soothed merely by being in his presence. As he works away at whatever challenge this morning has brought him, I ponder our quandary about Stella. In everyday terms this placement is a great success: her reactions to all of the family members, her behaviour and willingness to fit in with all of us, her fascination with all our routines and the ups and downs of family life, and how lovely it is to see little signs of confidence – like with the choosing of the cake in The Rose Garden, and the little embellishments she is making to her clothing choices as she dresses herself every day. On paper, it is all working.

The reality is that something deeply disturbing is going on underneath.

Lloyd is preoccupied with his work so his replies are a bit curt. 'I agree. There is clearly more to it,' and, 'Yes, but you know that we can't rely on social workers always getting it.'

He's right, of course. As was WPC Watters in what she said. The social workers are too busy to have time to reflect fully on events: they spend so much time reacting to crises in a system that is tremendously high-pressured and shockingly under-resourced. I think again about how wrong the process is. Social workers are forced by the way their practice has become over the last few years to have a particular mindset that doesn't give them the head space to think things through.

Frustrated as I am with Debbie for not returning my calls, I am pretty sure she is dealing with an urgent situation – anything from a child who is refusing to get in a taxi after school, to an absconder who has gone missing, or a self-harmer. You name it, they live it daily, running from one emergency to another. Lloyd suffers my musings patiently, but I'm not helping any of us, and I'm not getting any work done, either.

The week goes by, the world keeps turning, Stella settles back down, and I still don't hear from Debbie. By now I am really desperate to speak to her. I am certain that we are missing something: that Stella is seeing or experiencing something we just can't see – because we cannot know – because we weren't there in her early life. At last, more than a week after the disastrous contact visit at the family centre, there is a message from Debbie. I go through the laborious

Egress system, and as her message appears I am at first, and untypically, lost for words. The expression 'I feel my blood boil' is the only way to describe the hot feeling that pulses through my veins and spreads around my body as I read: *Contact has been arranged for Thursday as per last week. Please ensure Stella is at the family centre at 5pm.*

No! No! No! Is she serious? Who in their right mind would do that given what happened last time? Clearly nothing that I have been saying has got through. I march into Lloyd's office, furious with the world and needing to share my fury, but he's busy on the phone and wags a warning finger at me. I curse him, too, even though he has done nothing wrong. I can't take her back to contact. Can't anyone see why this is not a good idea right now? Grinding my teeth at the injustice of all of this, I decide to take the dogs for another walk, even though we have not long returned from their morning's exercise. Perhaps it will ease some of my anger and outrage that I feel for this poor little girl, and expend some of the adrenalin and nervous energy that is coursing through my system.

Again, I find myself in the position of having to tell Stella that she has contact with her mum on Thursday. I am very gentle, in spite of everything that I feel. I watch her reactions closely.

This time it is different. She says nothing at all for a very long time. She doesn't look at me, but down towards the floor. One foot, in its dainty little school shoe, makes a determined circle on the floorboards. Then, in her tiny voice, that is usually so polite and compliant, she mumbles, very quietly, 'I don't want to.'

I know it has taken a very great deal for her to articulate that. It is a big sentence for this little, quiet girl.

And that's enough for me.

I email Debbie and cc Dave. I also text Debbie to ask her to check her email because Stella has expressed the view that she does not want to see her mum. I am determined. I could not be any clearer in tone and tenor. I also send an email to WPC Watters. Belt and braces, belt and braces.

Once again, I hear nothing whatsoever from Debbie. Where the hell is she? It's difficult to avoid the feeling that I'm being deliberately ignored. I remind myself again of the pressures that she is under.

But this can't go on. It really can't.

I decide to call Dave directly. I need some advice here. I need to talk to someone. All I know is that I don't want Stella to go through another upsetting contact. I get Dave straight away.

'Hi Dave, it's Louise Allen.'

'Yes, Louise. How can I help?'

I explain my concerns for Stella and my frustration that I have not heard from Debbie.

'Me neither. I've also been chasing her, and I just found out this morning that she is on sick leave.'

I blow out my cheeks in a deep sigh. That explains a few things, at least. 'But what about Stella?'

'I hear you, Louise. I'm waiting to hear from Debbie's manager about what to do.'

I say, and I know that I am sounding like a petulant child myself as the words come out, 'But contact is *tomorrow* and Stella is behaving in a way that sends out the clear message that she does not want to go!'

Dave tries to be soothing. 'I know that, and I trust your instincts. But we both know that we can't do anything without authority from the manager of the Looked After Child team. It's not our decision to make.'

I am not soothed. 'Don't force me! Don't make *me* make her do something she doesn't want to do!' I want to scream, and wonder afresh at how bureaucratic systems always seem to trump common sense. It doesn't matter if my instincts are trusted: a child is not being listened to. A child who already has no real voice is having their words drowned out once again. Again, I am furious.

He's right, though. I know he is. Our hands are tied. I have no choice but to take her to that contact visit.

I blow out another big sigh and swear profusely inside my head, a string of invectives; not out loud to Dave, though – I think he's a Christian.

Suddenly, it is already Thursday morning. I am wide awake, but there is still another half hour until the radio alarm is scheduled to go off. This always happens to me if I know that I really need to be somewhere: when I have an interview, or need to catch a train, or when we are going away on holiday. Today my first thought is for Stella. Her contact visit feels as though it is in that same out-of-the-ordinary, anxiety-inducing category of events. I tell myself that I'm over-reacting and that I need to get a grip, and then I remember the state that Stella was in when I picked her up from the first contact a fortnight ago.

Lloyd is still asleep, or so I think, until he sits up and with his eyes still closed he says, 'Stella?'

'Yep.'

We don't need to say anything else to each other. He knows what I am feeling. Since we first began fostering we have wasted many hours trying to understand the vagaries of the 'system' that we all call 'Children's Social Care.' The only conclusion that we regularly draw is that it's bonkers. I refuse to use the tired adage 'it is what it is' because I have to hold onto the belief that it *can* be different, that I can help to be an agent of that change, and that one day some sense will appear en masse into the system. I live in hope. It is the only way to get through.

It's another warm morning but I grab my dressing gown and tie it up firmly. I push open Stella's bedroom door; she is curled up with the pillow half over her head. This is not unusual. I have noticed that several of our foster children have slept with the pillow over their head: it must offer some sort of protective feeling, perhaps. The position that she is in gives the impression that she has disappeared right into the bedding somehow, but she looks comfortable. I leave her for a bit and let her sleep.

Downstairs I make two cups of strong coffee. I turn on the radio: all bad news. I turn it straight back off. I take the coffee back up to bed. Lloyd and I sit on top of the covers and talk about the hedge that needs trimming at the front, how ineffective the new washing powder is, whether it's time to check the guttering again. Tangible, practical things that we can control. We do this when we can't face another conversation about a foster child who, no matter what we do, gets fed through a system that is not concentrating.

I say goodbye to the other children once they are ready, do the usual call out list of 'have you got…?' and then close the front door on all the normal domestic disarray to walk with Stella to the car. She is quiet, even more so than usual, and squeezes my hand tight as we walk down the little road.

'Are you ok?' I ask, as brightly as I can.

'Yes, thank you, Louise.' She looks up at me as she says it and those big eyes reveal that she is anything but ok. This hurts more than I will ever show, because I know that she can't yet tell me what she is really thinking.

I remember responding in just that way to a nice teacher at primary school who strongly suspected I was being abused. I know that she wanted to help. She asked me if I was ok and I responded with an identical 'yes, thank you' to the one that Stella has just given me. It's easier for everyone, because how do you have the words to explain what you think when you are a child?

In the car I put Kiss FM on for her again. This time she just stares into space. I feel the hurt, her hurt, all over again; in training they call it 'secondary trauma'. Being around children who have themselves been traumatised makes us vulnerable to their pain. I don't know about that, but as a compassionate human being I feel terrible that later today I will be responsible for driving a little girl into a situation that she does not want to be in for reasons that she cannot explain.

The playground is bustling with the usual morning action: children meet their friends, find the right place to stand in line, dash back to departing parents for forgotten water bottles and lunchboxes and PE kits. I make a detour past all this and go with Stella directly to reception. I ask to see Stella's teacher. Mrs Griffiths comes along in just a few moments, brushing down her trousers. Her dyed blonde hair parted in the centre and slightly over-rouged cheeks give her the appearance of a rag doll, but one that is creased and worn in all the right places. I leave Stella sitting on a chair in the entrance while I apologise for disturbing what must be valuable preparation time for a teacher in the morning. Enthusiasm oozes from every pore of her being and I wonder how she keeps up the energy at this late stage in the term. I quickly explain that Stella has contact later on today and she may be a little quiet or unsettled given what happened last time.

Mrs Griffiths smiles warmly and says that 'we' will keep a close eye on her. She is fond of this inclusive pronoun, and sprinkles her utterances liberally with 'we'. 'We can't be worrying now, can we?' and 'We don't want to be drawing attention to…' I find myself almost turning around to see who the other person making up this 'we' is. But it is an endearing habit, and one that I find reassuring. In fact, 'we' like it very much. Apparently, we can always phone at lunchtime if we are still worried, just to check how she is getting on, if we want to. That makes me feel much, much better. It's not just me looking out for Stella today. Even though Mrs Griffiths is rather thin and angular, somehow she just exudes the feeling of a big, warm hug. She has the perfect demeanour for a primary school teacher.

Back home I update the log and send a quick email to WPC Watters to explain that Debbie is on sick leave. I leave out all reference to wishing that we had known earlier.

The day drags. I finish off number four of the 12 illustrations: now the colours have subconsciously become the colours of Stella, not just her yellow gingham dress, but her white socks and the sparkly turquoise hair clips are there in an abstract way, too.

I pop into Lloyd's office where we talk about a piece of work. Anything to avoid discussing the shadow of contact that still overhangs the day. Eventually, as though it has been dragged there against its will, lunchtime arrives. While I stir the soup, I call Stella's teacher. Miss Griffiths is honest. She informs me that Stella has been quiet and definitely preoccupied. 'We' didn't want to eat anything, nor did we want to join in with our friends at playtime.

I thank her for this. I am more convinced than ever that I have to stop the contact. I can do nothing else but call Dave. He lets me know that he has managed to speak to Debbie's manager but the news is not good. We need to go ahead with contact – everyone is at this 'we' business, now, it seems. It's too late to cancel the contact worker, or Shannon, who apparently has to catch a bus to the family centre.

Just after 1pm I start the draft for illustration number five. My client liked the simple but bright colours that I sent off this morning for the first four images, but right now I feel dull inside. Consequently, the colours have faded. I know that Stella is holding all the trauma that has ever happened to her deep inside, and that she is scared because of her mum. What else can 'we' do? Not much. I call Rita, the contact worker at the family centre, and let her know my concerns, mostly because it's something to do. I ask her if she can be even more vigilant than usual. I know this is not the correct protocol, but I can't go through the correct protocol because it takes too long and nobody answers and as far as I'm concerned this is an emergency: it's Stella's emergency.

Listening to the afternoon play on the drive over to Stella's school does little to help take my mind off contact: it's all about an ex-convict who is trying to build relationships with the people he hurt. My head is bursting with compassion for Stella. Sometimes I feel cross and I know that it isn't 'secondary trauma', it's my own first-hand experience. Empathy can take you so far – and of course, many teachers and social workers are brimming with empathy – but this doesn't mean that they can truly understand the anxiety that Stella is experiencing right now. If they did, she would not be going to contact.

I am standing right by the classroom door in the playground when the bell rings to signal the end of the day. Stella creeps out of the door like a little ghost. Miss Griffiths attempts to talk to me, but is ambushed by two mothers in dispute about a school jumper. I smile and wave. Stella is also smiling and waving, bravely. I hold her hand and she returns the little squeeze that I give it. We are letting each other know we're here.

I park the car near The Rose Garden with a terrible sense of deja vu. I make faux jolly chatter as we sit down at a table. I suggest she looks at the cakes; this time she says she isn't hungry. I suggest a milkshake, but it sits in front of her and she makes no attempt to touch it. I half drink a cup of tea, desperately trying to contain my anger at this utterly ridiculous situation. We still have 45 minutes until the scheduled contact time, and I don't know how to fill it. I know there is a little park a few roads away from the family centre, but I decide against it just in case Shannon is early and Stella sees her coming in. We drift along the shopping parade browsing in the charity shops again until it's time.

Stella walks slowly, dragging her feet. The little fairy child is momentarily gone: there is nothing light and airy about the way she is moving today. I have a *Thelma and Louise* moment: what if I just pull the plug on this whole charade and walk away with Stella, choose not to put her through what is clearly becoming an unpleasant ordeal? But the rational side of me returns: I know that I can't, because I would get into trouble for non-compliance. It would go onto my record and ultimately be damaging for Stella and for future children that we might care for. Shannon could make a complaint against me.

And this is where being called a foster 'parent' is so wrong, such a misnomer. If I was allowed to actually behave like a parent then I would not be here. I wouldn't choose this. No one who loves Stella would put her through this.

Rita meets us in the entrance to the family centre. I put my arm across Stella's shoulder. 'If you feel upset or want to come out at anytime, you just tell Rita.'

Rita follows my lead like she knows the script. 'That's right, Stella. If you feel unhappy at any time and want me to phone Louise to come and get you, just tell me. Ask to speak to me. I am right by you.'

I watch them walk towards the double red doors with the matching long steel handles. Stella turns around and gives me a little wave, before the doors swallow her up and clang shut.

I feel sick. I go to the car and wait. No radio, no texting, no nothing. My phone is on and ready if Rita calls. I don't want to be distracted for even a moment. I am ready to leap into action.

The car clock flashes at me accusingly. Five minutes pass, then eight. 10 minutes, 12 minutes. Sitting here is excruciating. And I have to remind myself that however bad it is for me, it is likely to be much worse for Stella. An elderly couple walk across the car park. They have a little fluffy terrier with them. If Stella was in the car I would say, 'Look Stella, fluffy dog,' and she would say 'Awww, cute,' and wave her hands about with joy. I play out the conversation in my head as though she is safely in the car with me and wonder if this is a first sign of madness.

17 minutes. The phone rings: it's Rita.

I fly towards the entrance where Rita is standing with Stella, who is crying. I look beyond them through the round window of the double red doors to see a woman with long blonde hair: Shannon. We lock eyes for a tiny moment.

I take Stella by the hand and reassure her that we are going straight home.

To Rita I mouth a request to see if I can call her later.

She nods, and her eyes are serious. 'I'll be free to talk this evening, Louise. Whenever you're ready.'

As I help Stella into the car I give her a huge hug. 'It's all over.'

Though I know, really, that it is not. And I am haunted by the image of Shannon that I caught through the window. There was deep concern on her face, but it wasn't directed at Stella, it was directed at me: concern about what, though?

Chapter 8

The car journey home is very subdued. Stella doesn't talk very much anyway, and it seems that the last thing she wants to do is speak about what has just happened. I don't want to push her. I try really hard to just focus on keeping everything as normal as I possibly can. Though it's not normal to dread seeing your own mother and then flee from that situation in distress for an unseen reason.

Lloyd is surprised that we are back so soon, but I shake my head. I can't talk to him and go through what's happened yet. Food. A snack. I offer the contents of my kitchen cupboard. Stella asks for a sandwich and a packet of crisps. This is good because it means that she is feeling better, safer. I suggest to Lily that after Stella has finished eating they both go and play or watch a film together. Lily can sense something is up and drags her heels because she wants to know what's happened, too. I shoo them both out of the kitchen with a bag of popcorn and two bowls to share it out. That does the trick.

A bemused Lloyd gets the very abbreviated version of events. What I really need to do is to talk to Rita. He waits patiently while I make the call. She answers within three rings. My eyes swivel towards the door and Lloyd understands, moving swiftly to prevent the girls from hearing.

'Hi Rita, can I put you on speaker phone? Do you mind? Lloyd needs to hear this conversation too.'

'Sure, no problem.'

I can tell that she is at home: I can hear *The One Show* on in the background as she gives her account of the meeting. Again, there doesn't seem to be much to say. Shannon was kind and gentle. She did not impose herself onto Stella in any way. 'Frankly, Louise, I'm baffled by Stella's reaction.'

I ask Rita to talk me through blow-by-blow exactly what happened. I am determined to get to the bottom of this.

'Stella was sitting next to me on the sofa, and Shannon was on the opposite sofa.'

I interrupt to ask what she was wearing. Rita obliges with a description of Shannon's pale grey hoodie, complete with pink letters on the front. Perhaps it's the hoodie that has triggered a memory. 'Was she wearing that last time?

Rita struggles to remember, and, in fairness, this is way beyond her remit.

'Most of the parents who come into the centre are wearing hoodies and jeans; it's practically a uniform.'

I laugh to lighten the mood. But what else does she remember?

'She looked clean and tidy, but she did smell of cigarettes again.'

Is it as simple as that? I wonder if the smell from Shannon is the trigger to past trauma. Maybe both parents smoke?

We are both churning over every detail. Rita humours my forensic analysis; she knows how important this is. But she also volunteers the unwelcome information that after the meeting, Shannon said that she was terribly worried about Stella. That there was such a deterioration in her emotional stability. She even suggested that Stella had never done anything like this before – until she came to live with us.

Great. So, Stella's reactions are our fault now. Here we go. We've been here before. Lloyd and I are, sadly, used to accusations from birth families. It's often a mix of anger, shame, and sometimes other mischief, as I suspect is the case here. She is sowing the seeds to suggest that there is something deficient in our care of Stella.

I move on. That part can be dealt with later. It's a nasty side effect of what we do, but not unexpected.

'Did Stella and Shannon do anything together?'

Rita speaks slowly, reliving the scene. 'Shannon took a book from the box by the sofa and opened it out on the table to read with Stella and look at the pictures.' I wonder which book it was – perhaps the emotional reaction has something to do with the content of the story.

'*The Smartest Giant in Town*, I think, and then another one, an animal one, I'm pretty sure, something about rabbits.'

We have that Julia Donaldson book upstairs. I can check through it later. Sounds harmless enough, but you never know. Rabbits, though, could be anything. Once again I feel like a television detective stumped during a difficult-to-solve case. Just the vastness of possibilities out there, and the impossibility of hitting on the right one.

'Do you want me to check on the rabbit book? I can have a look when I'm back at the family centre and see if I can work out which one it was.'

'Maybe. You never know. It could be relevant.'

Rita continues: 'Then I think Shannon got some biscuits out of her bag. We encourage families to bring food to help soften the experience. It was right then that Stella began crying and asking for you.'

Lloyd and I look at each other. This is just not making any sense.

I ask what Shannon had brought in for snacks.

'Wait. It was a packet of cheese biscuits and a Lion Bar, I think.'

That's it! My mind is racing: Lion Bar. Lion Bar. That's the trigger. I took a Lion Bar out to the garden with some drinks the first day that Stella became really upset. It's something to do with that particular brand of chocolate. It has to be.

'Thank you, Rita. You are a star.'

Rita has no idea quite why she is a star, but I am certain that she has helped to unlock the mystery. I finish the call as

Lloyd looks at me with his 'What are you doing now?' face. I usually ignore it.

Tonight I have a new energy as I write up my logs. I also email WPC Watters with the start of my hypothesis about the Lion Bar. I can almost hear Dave saying, 'Slow down, Louise,' over my shoulder as I type – as he inevitably would if he were with me in the room. He has a way of making me feel like an excitable child. But I want to get to the bottom of this to help Stella, and I have a feeling that WPC Watters will support my line of investigation.

I sleep better than I did the previous night, after churning over several ideas and explanations; none of them are nice.

In the morning I take Stella to school as usual. Routine and normality are key to her getting through this. I remind her that it's Friday: we love Fridays in our house, and make a point of marking the end of the working week with a bit of a celebration. Because Lloyd and I both work from home, we really enjoy the freedom of being able to officially stop on our own terms, when we decide. We aim to finish early on a Friday, whatever pressing deadlines may be out there. We cook together and chat, and the children relax, eat treats and have a lovely time along with us. They all like the Friday feeling, and the anticipation of it, too – and Stella has quickly absorbed this.

Helping the Friday feeling is the fact that my mood is much more upbeat now that I feel I have the start of an answer. I will fight hammer and tongs to ensure that Stella does not have to go back to contact. I think my good humour helps Stella, too, though so much is unsaid. I hope that somehow she is recognising that I am going to protect her with my life – because she matters and is worth the fight.

On the way to school, we sing along to our usual radio station. I can almost hear her voice this time and, more importantly, I can see that magic little smile.

I catch Mrs Griffiths at the door and quickly feed back that contact didn't go well. Her mouth forms a grim line and she comments that maybe now 'they' will stop it. I can feel some of my own frustrations in the vehemence with which she says the words, and I guess that sometimes the relationships between schools and children's social care can also be problematic.

On the way home, I call into the supermarket. I have a few groceries to buy, which I select quickly, and then I head for the confectionary aisle, where I stand for an age in front of the wall of sweets and chocolate. My eyes scan the offers, as they always do, alert for those little red labels that tell me what a bargain I am getting. I tell the children that shopping for offers is a way of trying out new things and saving money. The fostering allowance is small, so clever budgeting has become an important and necessary part of being a foster carer. My sons have commented that since I gave up my full-time job and started fostering we don't visit certain upmarket supermarkets anymore. I miss them too, but 'we are where we are', as the saying goes – anyway, I'm much happier and just have to be a little more creative in my desire to suggest abundance. It is, perhaps, a little unorthodox – and I certainly haven't mentioned it to anyone officially – but I decide to try an experiment: tonight I will put a number of different chocolate bars out for the children to choose from. Into the mix I will add a few Lion bars. I need to understand if my nascent theory about Lion bars has any value in relation to Stella's behaviour.

For dinner I cook a homemade sweet and sour chicken with rice. Lily has the same meal, but hers is not cooked with meat. I am becoming a dab hand at starting off a dish in two different pans and thereby only having to chop one set of ingredients. The atmosphere is easy and relaxed and I'm pleased about that: the conditions are perfect. After dinner, and when their food has had time to settle, I call them all in to choose a bar of chocolate. I watch Stella carefully. She loves chocolate and is quick to arrive in the kitchen. On the table they lie: Snickers, Topics, Milky Way, Maltesers – all the usual suspects – and then the Lion Bars right in the middle. The children pile in to make their choices with gleefully shouted thank yous, but Stella stands back and looks very unhappy.

I swallow. This is hard, but I have to know. 'Stella, shall I move the Lion Bars away and put them in the bin?'

It is a moment of truth. She nods, quickly. Jackson and Vincent watch in utter disbelief as I put three perfectly good Lion Bars into the kitchen bin. Has their mother finally gone mad? I suspect they may be rooting around in the rubbish a bit later. Stella looks relieved, and with a cheeky look, helps herself to two bars from the table.

I smile.

That evening I decide to just email WPC Watters with a summary of my 'findings'. Within a few minutes of sending it, my phone goes. WPC Watters wants to hear all about this evening's chocolate experiment. I offer my idea that the Lion Bar is somehow operating as a symbol for something quite serious that is frightening to Stella.

She is quiet for a moment on the other end of the phone. Then she explains that sometimes abusers are known to control their victims with a word, or an object, that is known only to them. She has a strong suspicion that this is what may be going on in this case, and asks if it would be okay to pop round in the morning to have another little chat with Stella. I'm impressed with the urgency, but surprised that she wants to come tomorrow – a Saturday. The social workers will not be working. Then I wonder if that is precisely the reason that Saturday has been chosen, so that WPC Watters has freedom to investigate without hindrance.

It's late morning when she arrives. Again, there isn't the whiff of institution about her. This time she is dressed simply in jeans and a white shirt covered in butterflies of many colours and designs. I don't know how she is able to look so relaxed and untroubled, knowing what we both suspect. The slime is out again – it's such a fad at the moment. In the kitchen both girls are busy adding glitter and food colouring to their individual concoctions. WPC Watters insists now that we call her 'Julie'. I'm pleased, because it sounds much friendlier, and also because 'WPC Watters' was quite a mouthful. Julie spends plenty of time engaging with the girls, as though she is an ordinary friend of mine who has popped in for a casual natter on a Saturday morning. There is no hurry, no sense of agenda. Dotty and Douglas have decided that Julie is acceptable, and even Pablo Picasso jumps up to be stroked, recognising a calming influence.

Lily breaks off a lump of slime for Julie to play with – a generous gesture on Lily's part, to willingly sacrifice some of the precious gloop. Julie joins in their games with ease and humour, moulding her slime into all sorts of animals and goofing around as much as the children are. I set two cups of tea down on the table, well away from the slime, and make up soft drinks for the girls. Some of yesterday's chocolate remains, so I ask the girls if they would like a bar. Stella looks uncomfortable; I notice Julie observing her and know that she sees it too. Two harmless Milky Ways find their way to the kitchen table. Stella's relief is palpable and she tucks in.

After a little while, I take the nudge from Julie to move Lily and myself out of the kitchen. She does it very subtly – a little look is enough. We leave them alone together. I take Lily to the sitting room, intending to do some housework, but find myself unable to get stuck into anything more productive than some half-hearted dusting and re-piling of books and newspapers. I hear the electric drill going upstairs. Lloyd has decided that now is the moment to put up the new pelmet in the guest room. The buzzing sound of the tool creates a sense of industry and purpose that's good for a Saturday, when a lot has to be done. It also prevents me in practical terms from earwigging any of the conversation that is going on in the kitchen, as I might otherwise be tempted to do. I tell myself that I'm not annoyed by this.

Eventually Julie comes into the sitting room and asks Lily if she would like to carry on sliming with Stella as her hands are worn out, and thanks her for being patient.

'Another cuppa?' I ask Julie, pointedly.

'Definitely!'

As we sit down in the sitting room I apologise for the sound of the drill in the background and the odd, loud expletive coming from the guest room as Lloyd struggles with the business of making holes in our very old walls. Julie laughs. But that is more than enough small talk for me.

'Is there any basis to my theory around the Lion Bar, then?' I need to know what she has discovered. 'Being a symbol for something darker, as you suggested?'

'Absolutely. Well done, Louise. You were spot on in your assumptions.'

I feel a sudden mix of triumph and sadness. It is what I wanted to hear and I'm happy to have helped uncover the mystery, but at the same time it's also exactly what I dreaded hearing.

Julie goes on, 'It seems that mum uses the Lion Bar as a way of controlling Stella. We don't know exactly what it stands for, but as you have seen, Stella is terrified by it. Given the way that Shannon has gone about things, I would imagine that she wanted to see Stella and arrange contact solely to ensure that Stella doesn't disclose the abuse that has evidently been going on.'

She pauses to let me take all of this in. It is not exactly the first reason you might hope that a mother would have for meeting up with her child, and no wonder that Stella's anticipation of the contact visit changed so dramatically between the first and the second time.

'I know it's hard to believe, but it's quite common, sadly,' Julie explains.

And then she starts to use words like 'child pornography' and 'paedophilia'. She is using them very generally and doesn't mention Stella's name, but I know that she is inviting me to make the connection for myself. I also know that I had already known this deep down – the evidence has been presented before my eyes, but it's still a shock to hear an officer of the law say it out loud. Something jars in my memory. I remember the teacher's note about that first time Stella got changed for a school PE lesson, written up in her case file: *Class teacher raised a concern during Stella's first PE lesson. Stella stripped off completely, folded her clothes into a neat pile and then stood entirely naked, for all to see.*

I have looked after children who have been sexually abused who strip off and display behaviours that might be deemed sexually provocative, and exhibitionist – running around naked and sticking their bums in the air – but they haven't had the quiet dignity of Stella. That teacher noticed something odd when Stella got herself ready: Stella standing naked but composed, in expectation of something.

'Yes, that would definitely be consistent with what we are starting to piece together,' says Julie when I tell her what I have remembered, 'and is perhaps further evidence of the systematic nature of what was happening.'

'Observant teacher,' she adds a beat later.

We both pause again, before Julie continues, 'And we have had a number of other cases where *after* the abuse has taken place the child is 'rewarded' with a bar of chocolate. The abuser knows that if they use the same chocolate, or whatever the reward is, it will become a form of control: a reminder to stay silent – or else. It's quite deliberate and systematic. Stella had built up enough trust in you to be able to express her fear, which is really important. She showed you what was going on. You should feel good about that. Some children never let on.'

Yet I feel anything but good. I feel numb. I am devastated. Sweets, chocolate, treats, saying 'cheese' for a photo: these are all innocent childhood things – or at least they should be. In the hands of an abuser they are used against the child as a form of control and manipulation. It is so, so warped and wrong. I sit totally still on the sofa, oblivious now to the sound of Lloyd's drill in the background, unable to touch my tea. Then I hear Lily and Stella singing in the kitchen, and it brings me back to a kind of reality. But the world makes no real sense to me in this moment. Child abuse makes no sense.

'Did Stella tell you what…?' I leave the sentence unfinished.

Julie goes on to explain her suspicions that Shannon was selling Stella to men in her home. Again, she gives me a moment to digest this.

'And I strongly suspect, especially after the 'say cheese' incident, combined with the headteacher's evidence, that they were photographing and filming Stella. Naked − or participating in sexual acts with other children or adults.'

I feel myself sink further and further into the chair. How can this even *be*? I am screaming inside, while I gently sip my tea and hear a little girl singing in the next room. I want to tear apart these people who have hurt Stella, such a gentle, blameless child.

I hear myself asking questions that I don't think I actually want to know the answer to. 'How do they get children to perform sexual acts on each other?'

'Coercion,' she responds, quickly. 'It doesn't take a lot to control a child, especially one who has been brought up to know little else. It's likely that there would have been a Lion Bar placed by them as a warning that if they don't do exactly as they are told then they would get it.'

I notice the specifics of the Lion Bar but the anonymous 'them.' I don't think either of us can fully confront the reality of this happening to Stella.

I ask what 'get it' means.

Julie looks down into her cup. 'It can be a beating – or a violent rape. Maybe the threat of someone they love being hurt. Whatever it takes.'

There is simply nothing to say to this. *Whatever it takes.* We both sit quietly for a few minutes while Julie allows me to process the news. I keep thinking about Stella's little hands, her little bony legs, every part of her that has been exploited, used. She is so small and undernourished and totally vulnerable.

My own tears are rare, these days. I seem to have strangely few left to spare for the world after surviving my own childhood horrors, but I find them flying freely from me now. Julie passes me her handkerchief. It's only injustice like this that seems to make me cry these days. Injustice to children.

'So. What happens next?' I force myself to ask, determined to focus on the future for Stella now, and not dwell on an ugly past.

Julie says that she has more than enough information to start an investigation, and that Stella will probably stay in care.

It hasn't occurred to me that she wouldn't – that she could yet be sent back – but apparently that is what has been requested by Shannon.

'There is little in Stella's file about her history, as you know, but I have some other lines of enquiry to follow up: some colleagues in Stella's father's area who might be able to supply more information and help.

'But what happens to Stella in the meantime? We can't leave her like this with all these loose ends.' I'm feeling helpless again. I don't have other 'lines of enquiry' to follow, just a damaged child in my house.

Julie talks about a programme for children run by specialists who will work with Stella.

'And how long will that be for?'

'In an ideal world, for as long as it takes.' She takes a long look at me. She knows that I am not naive. 'But with the current cutbacks, who knows?' She touches my arm. 'But she has us, remember. Between us, we'll be advocates for her.'

It's not enough.

I know what living with the stain of abuse is like. I hate the idea that Stella is going to live with the same dirt clinging to her all her life. The world expects a lot from abused children: it wants them to just fit in. They have every right not to, but what is the alternative if they can't sustain education, relationships and jobs? The outlook is not good.

Julie interrupts my thoughts. 'I'll call a strategy meeting with the relevant professionals straight away. We need a strategy around Stella to protect her, and I need to launch the investigations proper.'

I know that as a policewoman she is almost certainly not sharing all of her inside information. In Julie's line of work she may well already know of characters who might be connected to Shannon and Stella. That's her job. And she is welcome to it. My job is to help this little girl back into the world, somehow.

My head is in a spin but as a veteran of the world of abuse, resilience is my familiar. I know how it goes; it is like this. First there is pain. This is followed by rejection. And then, for many of us, there is survival. We live in constant survival mode. That's what we do. Only some of us have learned to really fit in. I hope that Stella can be one of the ones that makes it.

Chapter 9

For a few days afterwards we manage to carry on as normal, while waiting to hear from anyone from Children's Services about Stella. Julie has assured me that she will keep me updated, and I believe her, so there is nothing much else to do but wait. I have absolute conviction in her powers. Julie is clearly highly trained and very skilled at her work, and has managed to put together enough from Stella to pursue an investigation, so I'm confident that there are machinations behind the scenes, and progress is being made, even if I cannot see it.

We are enjoying something of an Indian summer; the early autumn is amber and hot. It seems a shame that the children are stuck back in classrooms while the sun is out. There were too many wet days during the holidays, but now the weather is set fair once again for the weekend. It's 6am on Saturday morning and I am on my second black coffee after hanging the first load of washing on the line. I have watered the pots by the back door and picked up all the dog mess: it is the curse of the dog owner that one of the first actions of the day inevitably involves the collection of poo.

Chores complete for the time being, I'm sitting on the bench inhaling the aroma of the fabric conditioner that wafts my way from the washing line. No matter how it's packaged and marketed, and what exotic scent is promised on the bottle, it does always end up smelling like 'fabric conditioner'. Nevertheless, I like it. Just as with my organised airing cupboard, fresh clean laundry has always given me a sense of being safe and grounded. I watch the children's clothes gently moving in the morning breeze and enjoy the fact that they will not need ironing.

When we began fostering, a few years ago now, I stopped ironing entirely. This was completely out of character. Even when I was a post-punk art school rebel I took great care of my clothes and my appearance, and have never been easy with being scruffy. I spent years washing and ironing and neatly folding every item of clothing, each tea towel, and all of the bedding. Then one day I heard myself saying to a good friend (who is Danish and has a hippy ease about her) that I enjoyed seeing my sons go off to school with crisp lines in their gleaming white shirts. I remember seeing her face and having a sudden epiphany that my sons couldn't give a hoot about how carefully their shirts were ironed and were going to get them dirty anyway.

I gained the four hours a week that I would have dedicated to ironing back, and spent them in the garden.

It gives me far greater pleasure. Now I specifically look for clothes that can get away with not being ironed. After I've finished pondering all these great philosophical thoughts, I go into the kitchen and see the fade from my phone leaving a message on the screen.

It's from Suzanna – a fellow foster carer and good friend. I number her amongst a group of us who have become very close, but who probably would never have met if it had not been for fostering. We met through turning up at the official carers' meetings and had the uncomfortable shared realisation that there were more social workers and staff than foster carers in attendance.

It soon became clear that none of us felt comfortable talking about the reality of the foster carer role in that environment. We quickly formed our own informal group that met up in the evenings with bottles of wine and good food and the intention to 'let it all out'. We can be a lively bunch when we get together, sharing our sometimes surreal, sometimes sad but always amazing stories and scenarios. It is far more productive than sitting in a community room with rubbish coffee and the same old biscuits, while having to take it in turns to speak for a regulated amount of time. These days it has morphed into one of the ubiquitous group chats on WhatsApp; but today's message has come privately.

Suzanna and her husband, John, need to go away at short notice. Derek, her husband's father, lives alone somewhere just outside Derby, and has suffered a fall that has left him with a broken shoulder. They look after three girls, Ellie, Tess and Chrystal, whom I know well and have a good relationship with. They, like most foster children, are dealing with 'stuff' and that can make their behaviour challenging. Suzanna has fought hard to try and get counselling for all the girls, but times are hard and there is little or no money to offer children in their position. Therefore she, like us, relies heavily on her own rather than the 'official' networks for support, and would naturally rather our children stayed with people they know. Local authorities and independent fostering agencies have diminishing pools of foster carers to draw on when someone needs respite. It can be easy to fall into the trap of never taking a break – not that visiting an ailing relative can really be considered as a break.

Having a break is important. Everyone needs the opportunity to relinquish responsibility and recharge their batteries once in a while, but it can be difficult to organise without going on a guilt-trip at the same time. A few years ago, Lloyd and I were told that if we didn't take a new child in placement on our family holiday (that had already been booked long before his arrival) then the placement itself would be in jeopardy – we would unwittingly be the cause of a placement 'breakdown'.

What was really happening was that our social worker at the time was also going on her holiday and didn't want the extra work of finding respite for the child in our care.

The child had only been with us for a day when we were told, in no uncertain terms, that he must accompany us. We spent a stressful two weeks getting hold of a passport and rearranging a villa with an extra room. We ended up paying a lot of money to take a child abroad whom we had just met. The holiday itself was a nightmare: the child was freaked out and overwhelmed by the experience. Not his fault, but consequently, he made our lives hell. Our family holiday was destroyed as we dealt with incidences of self-harming, defecation, absconding, stealing and a lot of anti-social behaviour. We came home drained and traumatised by the whole thing.

When we complained to our social worker that the family holiday had been a disaster, we were suspended from caring for six months. 'Respite' is a touchy subject for foster carers even if we call it 'sleepovers'.

I call Suzanna to get a clearer picture and find out what we might be letting ourselves in for. She sounds stressed.

'I know it's a big ask, Louise.'

Inside I think that the last thing I want for the start of this beautiful weekend is for the peace of it to be shattered with the arrival of three girls. Stella needs routine and normality and calm. But, somehow, I hear myself telling Suzanna that it's 'no problem'. I know that I'm saying yes because I am aware of what this means to my friend. Suzanna has limited options. It can actually be very difficult to leave foster children with friends or family because they need to have been DBS checked and approved. A big ask at the best of times, and impossible to arrange at short notice. Her relief is audible down the telephone.

We go through the necessary detail. Suzanna's girls all have different social workers. Two of them are fine – helpful and extremely supportive – but Chrystal, the newest arrival, has a social worker who seems to create problems. Suzanna describes her as a bit of a 'stick in the mud'. The other social workers are happy for the girls to come here and have what will feel like a big sleepover, but Chrystal's social worker wants Chrystal to have her own room. She does not approve of foster children sharing rooms with other foster children.

There is so much risk in this sector, so risk-aversion is key. Social workers and their managers are terrified of prosecution, but ironically, this uptightness can create more problems than it solves – as it is doing now. It's an attitude that drives me nuts. But we have extra rooms in our house because when we bought our wreck – sorry, 'project' – it was described in the estate agents' details as a 'mansion'. The description always makes us laugh, but quietly we quite like that idea of living in a mansion, however far removed that might be from the reality. It means that we have enough room to be able to accommodate the request: Suzanna can happily tell the social workers that the girls will have individual rooms.

'One last thing: can I drop them over shortly, so that they can have breakfast with you? That will mean we can get straight on the road before much of the weekend traffic.'

In for a penny, in for a pound, as the saying goes.

I go up to break the news to Lloyd that the girls are coming over for the whole weekend and will be here in a minute. He likes the girls, and they adore him; he is also well aware of my capacity for making spontaneous decisions, so he isn't surprised and it's not a problem. Lloyd has two grown-up daughters himself and is familiar with – or perhaps resigned to – having a houseful of young women. He asks what we are going to do for the day.

'Go to the beach,' I say. The words are out of my mouth before I have really had a chance to think through the logistics of all of this.

He raises a sleepy eyebrow. 'Good luck with that.'

I deny the girls their usual Saturday morning lie-in and wake them up to give them the good news about what's in store for the day. They are, predictably, very excited – both by the arrival of the girls and the promise of a trip to the seaside. Lily organises the packing of a beach bag with multiple towels and swimsuits.

The boys, however, are less enamoured of the plans and when I ask if they would like to come to the beach along with the girls the response is, 'No thanks, mum. You're good.'

Actually, I am relieved rather than disappointed at this decision. Jackson, who used to throw himself into the waves with such recklessness and inhibition, tends now to sit huddled self-consciously in a hoodie, not wanting to be noticed. Gone is the careless abandon as he approaches teenage life. So, fine. We will have a carload of girls.

Happily, Stella has already met Suzanna's girls when I took Lily and Stella to Suzanna and John's house just a few weeks ago. They have a smallholding that I have exploited on many occasions as a petting zoo for foster children, and knowing Stella's love of animals, it was a good activity for her to enjoy when she was first in the unfamiliar environment of our home.

Stella is closest to Tess, who she hit it off with more or less immediately. Although Tess is actually 11 years old, in emotional maturity she is more like Stella's age of five. This is not uncommon. Traumatised children have their own years. I sometimes think of it a bit like dog years: the chronological age means very little to a child who has not really had a childhood. Ellie is eight but is more like a two-year-old. She has global delay, which Suzanna thinks was caused by her mum being too depressed to look at her or nurse her. She was basically left in a buggy until she was six and had not started school by that age. Her walking is a little wonky, as are most of her gross motor skills, which can make her clumsy. Chrystal is 15 – going on four years, and sometimes 44 years. Her father has significant learning issues and had been trying to raise Chrystal by himself. He, along with a number of others in the region and beyond, had been exploited by a group of men who targeted parents with similar learning issues in order to gain access to their children. Vulnerable parents were manipulated to pimp out their children. Chrystal was left in her bedroom to be abused by men while her dad thought he was doing the right thing. Thankfully, some good policing blew this particular ring apart, but the numbers of children who have been affected in this way is horrendous. I know a few other carers who are looking after children who have been abused by this group.

Stella will be in interesting company, therefore, with these girls and this is part of the risk that Chrystal's social worker is concerned about. I take the view that I can manage the risk and at the same time try and let these children experience as much 'normal' as they can (though being in this sector over time has shown me that 'normal' is nothing much more than a setting on the tumble dryer).

Within half an hour my Saturday morning calm has utterly disintegrated. Having dutifully informed the social workers that all the girls will have their own rooms they have already, amidst squeals of excited delight, organised themselves with a big bundle of sleepover paraphernalia in Lily's room. Sleeping bags are set out on mattresses and beanbags. They love it. Oh well, I think. I suspect that Stella will end up in there too tonight.

The next milestone to negotiate is breakfast. I have catered for all tastes, knowing that for children like these, food is their politics. Croissants line up next to Rice Krispies, crusty rolls alongside Crunchy Nut Cornflakes, some fresh fruit and yoghurt. I appear to have somehow created a hotel breakfast buffet. Little Stella tries everything and is so polite, as usual. I suspect now that this is driven, in part, by fear, just as it was for me as a child.

While they tuck in to their various choices (more squeals, more noise, more laughter) I get on with packing the picnic. This one needs to cater for Lily's vegetarianism (that's her own version, the one where the vegetarian doesn't like vegetables or fruit and refuses to try anything new) but I have discovered Quorn mini scotch eggs, which have done the trick in recent weeks. Still, bearing in mind that what she liked yesterday may now be history, there are crisps and cheese straws and a quiche to try, too.

I smile to myself as the girls begin discussing possible ice cream flavours and making their selections for after lunch. We haven't even finished breakfast yet.

Given the number of my passengers for the day, I take our second car, the Citroen Picasso, which we bought from a friend of Lloyd's who owns a garage. It was a disability-adapted vehicle so came at a good price. It's one of those cars you drive to death, and years later, after two newer models of the car have been and gone in the marketplace, our trusty wagon just keeps on going. Glamorous it isn't, but I can make it into a seven-seater that leaves a spare seat for the picnic and beach stuff.

I say goodbye to Lloyd and the boys, sensing their joy in the realisation they have lost us for the day and can therefore do what they want. Lloyd gives me the 'What have you let yourself in for?' look, but there is no going back now.

Lily, who always likes to be different often just for the sake of it, decides that she will sit at the back all by herself

– on the far rear seat with the bags as company. I like to think that she may be doing this in part to be diplomatic. Chrystal, as the eldest, sits in the front next to me, and Ellie, Tess and Stella sit together in the middle. They pay absolutely no attention to my barrage of questions.

'Right then. Are you all ready?'

'Has everyone got everything?'

'Water bottles to hand?'

'Have you all done up your seatbelts?'

They are too busy laughing and gossiping and enjoying themselves.

I make a visual check that they are all securely strapped in, and hope for the best as far as everyone having everything they need goes. I am clearly now surplus to requirements as anything other than a chauffeur.

I reverse out of our parking area and hit the CD player, knowing already that it contains a summer song compilation that, it's fair to say, I was emotionally black-mailed into purchasing at the start of the summer while standing at the supermarket checkout.

When the boys were younger I used to make up CDs of all their favourite songs, a strange mix of 'Alvin and the Chipmunks' alongside Lou Read, Echo and the Bunnymen and the Eagles. It has been a while since I put one together.

Jackson had picked this one out while we were unloading the trolley onto the conveyer belt.

He said, plaintively, 'Our summer songs, mum.'

The CD had a load of tracks and artists that I had never heard of, but having not made a compilation for them in a while, I shoved it in alongside the rest of the groceries. It is fair to say that I am now far more familiar with the songs after a whole summer spent listening to them while ferrying the children around. So I resign myself to another 40 minutes of 'our summer songs, mum', the length of the drive to the beach. We are on the road just after half past eight in the morning.

The idea that the early bird catches the worm resonates well with me. All my life I have been an early riser, disliking staying in bed. I like to be up and doing things, which is one of the reasons that we achieve a good parking space close to the beach. I feel victorious!

I gather my little band of young women together. They carry a bag each, apart from Chrystal, whose sexual abuse has left her with traces of the prima donna about her. I understand that this actually results from the nature of the grooming process itself. She can be a bit of a madam, so I let her off and I carry her load as we head to the beach.

Just as with the parking, our early arrival has given us good choices of where to sit. I suggest a spot over by the beach wall. The girls all disagree for no reason other than they can. I head to the wall anyway and they all follow. I make a floor from blankets and line up all their towels and suntan lotions. Now the real exposure of me being with a group of fostered children is revealed. There is simply no comparison with what a 'typical' family or gathering of girls would look like. This is when I need a big sign that reads: *I am a foster carer. Do not judge us, please. Be kind.*

Chrystal has thrown herself down onto a blanket that she clearly has no intention of sharing with anyone. Instead of removing items of clothing to fit in with the beach ambiance, she is putting more layers on.

'Are you okay, Chrystal?'

There is no answer. I detect that very confusing mix of teenage emotions that make those years so difficult to deal with anyway, and then the other stuff: the baggage carried by a traumatised child, the things that I could never see or know about but can perhaps guess at from my own past experiences. But it could be anything that is bothering her right now: the design on a blanket? A few men sitting further away sunbathing in their trunks? A family that could resemble her own? Who knows? I am starting to suspect that we may not be spending as much time here today as I had hoped.

Lily is busy complaining about everything: the sand has got onto her towel. It's too hot. She can't walk across the pebbles because they hurt her feet. I refrain from pointing out that it is still quite early in the morning, so it will almost certainly get hotter, and of course there are sand and pebbles because we are AT A BEACH.

It's clear that Ellie will not leave my side; she is stuck to me like glue for some reason. I had brought a book and a magazine to occupy myself, rather optimistically imagining that they might all build sandcastles and paddle companionably in the sea while I relaxed. Both stay in my bag.

Tess and Stella are at least keen to get to the sea edge. Stella is wearing a swimming costume emblazoned with a glittery mermaid design. I have deliberately encouraged her to go for a one-piece rather than a bikini. I don't think there will be a repeat of the 'say cheese' incident, but a one-piece will at least give me more time to intervene. The day is already challenging enough without public displays of nudity thrown into the mix.

She is smothered in sun cream. They all are, but Stella particularly. That pale, nearly translucent skin clearly hasn't seen a great deal of sunshine, and I'm not taking any chances on that front. I wedge a sun hat on for further protection and good measure.

As I watch Stella approach the sea and run straight away giggling the minute the water touches her toes, it occurs to me that this may be the first time that she has seen the sea in real life. She is both bewildered by her surroundings and taking it all in her stride yet again. I am startlingly aware that I am surrounded by children who have not had the opportunity for childhoods.

To anyone watching us we are certainly an odd bunch. People might be thinking what a lot of rude and weird children, or that mother has no control over her flock; they have appalling manners. But I don't care. I'm working from a place where watching Chrystal smile – which she does for a fraction of a second when Stella tumbles into the waves – is one of the most moving events in my year. Seeing Lily eventually feel safe enough to sit down and enjoy 'being', after all the fears and anxieties that cause her to look like a stroppy child have abated, is a beautiful thing. To witness Tess running in the sea and laugh, apparently without a care in the world, while knowing what has happened to her, is joyful. Looking at little Ellie so totally absorbed in staring at a piece of a crab shell as though she can't quite believe in its existence is marvellous. And when precious little Stella plonks herself on my lap and squeezes her hot sweaty little body into my arms, I feel like I could cry with the emotion of it all. These girls have been through more than most adults could imagine. They will be judged and sidelined and even punished for what happened to them, but for now, while they are here in this moment, I hope they all remember that they have as much of a right to the good bits in life as everyone else.

Of course, the moment doesn't last for very long. Ellie announces that she has lost her glasses. Collectively, we turn the beach upside down. So many children in care seem to wear glasses, or have a lazy eye, or as we have seen all too frequently, rotting teeth. I pulled a rusty-looking nail end from Lily's mouth once, when she was younger, before I realised it was actually a tooth. We find Ellie's glasses eventually and a strange sort of peace resumes, though it is hard work keeping my little crew happy.

They argue, they laugh, they complain and push and shove and, eventually, after realising there is no way I can leave any of them on the beach while I go to the loo or get the ice-creams that have been discussed at length, I give up and we begin to pack our half-eaten lunch away. Experience has taught me that foster children will want those bits of food when least convenient, so I leave all possible nibbles at the top of the bag.

I get them to walk off the beach. There is more moaning about the pebbles. Stella and Ellie want to talk to every dog that walks by.

'Oh look. He's so cute!'

Invariably the dogs' patient owners allow all my party, including me, to fawn over their canine friends.

When we reach the promenade, Chrystal point-blank refuses to carry anything once more. She strops ahead on her phone, repeatedly shouting 'Fuck off' very loudly. Again, I wish I had that sign as I smile at passers-by with their alternately disapproving or pitying looks. Lily and Tess follow her lead and refuse to carry anything either. Lovely Stella tries to help, as does little Ellie. I feel my face heat up from frustration and shame, and sense further judgement for being a crap mother. *But I'm not any of these girls' mothers*, I want to shout. Their mothers aren't actually allowed to be alone with them.

Eventually we get back to the car. By now the beach has filled up and the prom is getting busy. I lug all the bags and blankets back to the car virtually single-handedly. The girls are still arguing and Chrystal is busy perfecting being a diva, but I remind myself that I understand why and accept that confrontation right now would be a disaster. 'Choose your battles carefully' is a mantra that most switched-on foster carers well know. I cling onto the joy in that moment on the beach from earlier.

As we reach the car, Lily leans against it and does her gentle head-banging action, a familiar way of signalling that she is fed up. Chrystal is still looking at her phone as a way of avoiding me and the others. I know she is embarrassed about her behaviour earlier but is unable to apologise or articulate her feelings. Grooming is a skilful and extremely dangerous, negative experience for a child. It clings to them for years, if not for ever. She is an incredibly manipulative child, because she herself was manipulated.

Tess is lying on the ground like a starfish, refusing to get in while making unintelligible 'uurrghhh' sounds and occasionally kicking the starfish legs up into the air. What a picture we make. Ellie is trying to run off and keeps jumping up the crumbling old stone wall in the car park. I wonder if we are ever going to make it out of this car park.

With trauma children I have noticed that if they are together they share their trauma behaviour, as though they almost enjoy the hysteria. Chrystal's rudeness and obnoxious attitude spread first to Lily, who often picks up and acts out the negative behaviours of our other foster children. She can be very tricky and refuses to hear me when I suggest that she has been influenced by other children, because she is convinced that she is more intelligent and above such antics – but she does it nevertheless.

Chrystal begins kicking her feet against my dashboard and I tell her to stop. She rolls her eyes and calls me a 'fucking bitch' under her breath but deliberately just loud enough for me to hear. I don't react, but then feel myself begin to heat up as Lily starts bashing about outside the car, criticising everything about the vehicle and moaning that Stella is sitting in her seat even though Lily made a point of sitting on her own at the back coming to the beach. Stella sits quietly until she's had enough, but then whispers to me that Lily is a bully and should sit in the back. I agree with at least the second part of that statement, which means that Lily then launches into a tirade about how I prefer Stella to her.

I notice that we have attracted more onlookers. Of course we have. This is good, free beachside entertainment. I wait for a bit, ignoring them. I try therapeutic de-escalation techniques, such as trying to talk the child down, but when you have four in a public space – and these children love an audience – it is not terribly successful. All of my foster children have enjoyed strutting around and giving it large when we're in public. They know they are safe.

I push away the 'why the hell am I doing this?' thoughts and try not to curse my lovely friend Suzanna. Instead, I slip straight into the adult who wants to be in control. I call on my old teaching voice that I used when I had a lecture theatre full of chatterboxes. It consists of a big 'ummmm' followed by my non-negotiable instructions.

'We need to get ourselves in the car and stop this display of poor behaviour.'

I add in a sharp 'NOW' when, after a fraction of a second, no one has moved – ever so slightly louder than I intended. Somehow Tess, Ellie and Lily all hop in, still quietly complaining and muttering and moaning, but with a new focus on getting out of here. The complaining is something that, over time, I have become fairly immune to, though sometimes it can get under my skin. I am determined that it will not today. The sun is shining, I remind myself. We return to the 'have you all got your seat belts on?' routine. Stella gives me two thumbs up as she rocks on her booster seat. Chrystal has pulled her long hair curtain-style across her face so she can't be seen. I start the engine and drive out of the car park and up the hill.

I am in the company of five young women who I am helping to grow up to be okay. I can do this.

But as we drive I hear myself speaking with the voice of the middle-aged exasperated mother-figure, the very person I never wanted to be. The person I avoided being as long as possible (I was 37 years old when I had my first child). Firm but friendly, I talk about how we all need to work together and not play a version of Trauma Mexican Wave, as it's pointless. Stella, my only fan left in the car during this awkward speech, says, 'Yes, Louise.'

I'm pleased – I also have to confess that witnessing her small act of rebellion against Lily just makes me sing inside with joy. She has always been so compliant.

As we get to the turning for the main road, a song comes on that I really love. Somehow I didn't realise it was on this CD.

As the music starts, I look in the mirror and see all the girls moving as if they are responding to some kind of primitive tribal call. Then come the lyrics to the verse. All about walking away from an unhealthy relationship – and not caring about what anyone else thinks.

They all wriggle into position. Chrystal lowers her phone and shakes back her hair, and then something amazing happens. From nowhere, they all start to fist pump and sing at the top of their voices as the song segues into its rousing chorus. I can't believe my eyes or ears as they all join in as one with the huge shout of 'I don't care!'

The moment is simply brilliant, and transcends everything that has gone before. I am driving along with the windows down, with five girls and, by now, me, all singing at the top of our voices. Our arms are waving, our hair is waving, there are people staring into the car perplexed, and I want a variation on my imaginary sign:

I am a foster carer and normally these children are busy making sense of their trauma but right now they're just having fun!

I put the track on repeat all the way home. They don't all understand all of the lyrics, but that doesn't matter. Nothing does. At this moment they really have no cares, and they love it. And so do I. The decibels in the car are off the scale. Even Stella has turned off the mute button and is yelling 'I don't care' from the top of her tiny lungs. Right here, right now, in this moment for these girls, nothing else truly matters. Not the past, nor the future; just now, here together in the car. Their cacophonous vocals are powerful and thrilling and I wish I could just bottle up this feeling for each of them – but especially for Stella – in the dark days that undoubtedly lie ahead.

When we get to our house they beg me to keep on driving to prolong the celebration. I can't bottle this, but I can give them one more go. So I wave carelessly to the house, and to a bemused Lloyd who is standing in the porch fixing up some wiring, and keep on driving with these energised, beautiful women singing for their lives. Their good lives. I can explain later.

Chapter 10

Dave is due for our monthly supervision on Tuesday. This will be a great opportunity for us to talk about Stella and what to do next for her.

Though Stella is still such a young child, only five years old, I think she knows on some sort of instinctive level that things are happening in the background – in the way that children do. I wonder if Stella has a sense now that she really is safe and that we, the adults, are working for her. I am optimistic that she is able to recognise that what she has here is different. I hope so, and I see signs of it. She seems to be able to move more and more towards the business of simply being a child. Day by day she seems more relaxed. Gone is the constant, careful watching that was so noticeable when she arrived. Now that I understand more about her past it occurs to me that she must have been sizing us all up and wondering if something untoward was going to happen to her at any given moment. We have looked after other children who have been sexually abused and if we have learnt anything, it is that each child lives with those experiences differently, and works things out in their own way. Some have been aggressive and angry, others have developed manipulative skills in order to survive, but little Stella seems to have a well of inner resources, an inbuilt programme that is steering her towards fitting in against the odds.

Television plays a big part in children's experiences and expectations, I know. The programmes that they watch are, inevitably, a form of modelling for adult life, a window onto a wider world out there. In my case, as a child, the world I saw on TV was the world that I wanted my life to be, so far removed from what it actually was. The definitive version for me existed in an iconic advertisement for Flake chocolate from the early 70s: a lady, casually dressed but well made-up, dreamily lifts her skirts to walk slowly through a poppy field, on the lookout for the perfect spot to sit and paint a watercolour. Her vibrant red hair and lipstick make her seem at home amongst the wild flowers. She settles down with her palette and mixes colours, before taking the inevitable, seductive chocolate break. It is a beautiful summer's day. Sunshine suffuses the whole image – until the rain begins. The raindrops smudge her painting, but she doesn't care because she has the chocolate – in fact, she seems pleasantly surprised by the effect that the rain has had on her work by the end. Not only do I still love the crumbliest, flakiest milk chocolate (even the lyrics are still there), but I myself became an artist who consciously adopted that attitude of optimism and ease – a Pollyanna-esque search for the 'good' in any situation, a focus on the value of the rain. Perhaps that evocative television advertisement filtered into my young, raw subconscious mind, so that I deliberately emulated the lady in the field. I know that at a similar age to Stella I wanted my life to be like the relaxed artist-lady.

No doubt Stella has her own version of the Flake advert, her own vision of what she would like life to be like – an inspirational woman, or a wholesome family playing together, perhaps. A way of holding onto the subliminal message that, even though she is trapped in trauma and its aftermath, something else is 'out there' for her. An alternative to her past – something that she can take control of herself, and achieve. The songs that she listens to on Kiss FM, the moving images that we're bombarded with every day, it could be anything: our world is saturated with better versions. Sometimes that can be harmful, but in a case like Stella's I think it might be uplifting.

As time passes and the days go by, Stella seems much happier. She does her drawings and can't wait to show me, or Lloyd, the fruits of her labours. She focuses on moments that she has enjoyed recently – pictures of herself playing with Lily, portraits of Dotty and Douglas, moments in the park. Lloyd makes a point of sticking her best drawing on the fridge so that she knows we can all see and admire it. It's part of the family gallery. We did this for our sons, who are both good artists, and for Lily, who also loves making pictures and things. It saddens me that recent educational policy appears to be squeezing out creative thinking and artistic activities: all the children we have ever looked after find a measure of absorption and comfort from being immersed in the absolute focus that 'making something' gives you.

She is eating well, too. Clears her plate entirely of the wholesome home-cooked meals that I strive to construct each evening, supplemented by plenty of fruit and raw vegetables.

I often put grapes or carrot sticks in a bowl by Stella and Lily when they are playing so they can have a healthy snack. These little details are important when you look after children who have not experienced the most basic aspects of good parenting on a regular basis. Sometimes they roll their eyes, especially the older ones, but they are smart enough to know that we mean well. I have always told our children and all the foster children that it is my job to get them to be good adults. I have to make sure they clean their teeth and wash properly. A big, white-toothed, healthy smile goes a long way for children who need to be able to make and keep good friends and eventually be able to live and work with other people, to become a good employee or a great boss. I tell them it all starts here. Every child, even the youngest ones, get that.

It's Monday morning, over a week later, before Stella broaches the question of her mother and contact visits again. We're driving to school, and the question pops out quietly.

'Do I *have* to see my mum?'

Even the phrasing of it makes my heart hurt – that plaintive 'have to.'

'NO!' My answer is loud and emphatic. 'You don't.' I have not squared this with Debbie or her manager, but I am not going to let that happen. If they want to give us a hard time, which I am ready for, I have WPC Julie Watters to back us up and plenty of evidence showing why it would be a bad idea.

She seems pleased. I know the complexity of the emotion, though. She will miss seeing her mum as well as enjoy the relief of not having to. It is never that cut and dried. But she's a smart girl and must know in the most primitive way that being apart from her mother gives her the emotional freedom to be herself. It won't stop her from saying or feeling that she loves her mum or parents, but there has to be an instinct for self-preservation, too. She knows which side her bread is buttered; why would she go straight back to something that wasn't working? That brought her pain and fear? It may take her many years to balance those books, though. It's a deeply complex issue, and it's a decision that has been made *for* her: a decision that is made for many children by the state, the corporate parent. It is never an easy one, but necessary for some in order to have the right to live without fear that *all* children should be entitled to.

After dropping Stella off at her school and running back into Jackson's school with the PE kit that he forgot this morning, despite the obligatory three reminders, I get ready for Dave's visit. Lloyd, as always, is busy chatting to clients in a virtual meeting. I always prefer meeting in the flesh, but Lloyd is very good with technology. He understands it and loves it and makes it work for him, in his domestic as well as his professional life. He can keep a good eye on what the children are doing on their devices, for example, where I wouldn't know where to begin. These days a parent or carer's technological skills have to be right up to date. I feel for adults who don't 'get' it. The children continue to move way ahead of us at astonishing speed. Managing output across multiple digital channels and apps to make sure that everyone is safe and appropriate is just a little bit different from being slightly more knowledgeable about the functions of the video recorder – which was my technological 'advantage' over the generation above in the 1970s.

Stella, thankfully, doesn't have access to a mobile phone, and even if she did, at her age I would have had a relatively easy conversation with Debbie and Dave about removing it. The Children's Act was written in 1989 and is now so out of date as to be positively unhelpful. There is no mention of technology – a beast that for parents and foster carers has become one of our biggest threats, but it's way down the list of things that need updating on a document that determines the circumstances under which we work as foster carers.

Dave has to drive from his office on the far side of our county. It usually takes him about an hour or so. We typically have our meetings in the morning, at ten o'clock. This suits me well: I am back from the school run, the dogs are walked and at least two loads of washing have been processed by that time. If I'm doing really well, then I have checked my emails and responded, too – which is the position I find myself in this morning when the doorbell goes and Dave's bulky silhouette shows through the mottled Victorian glass of the front door.

I lean into Lloyd's studio to let him know that Dave is here; he nods in acknowledgement and begins to wind up his part of the meeting, squeezing every inch out of his working day to allow time for this necessary, regular interruption.

I open the door to Dave, who clatters his suitcase noisily over the Victorian tiles in the hallway and then trundles it across the floorboards. He goes everywhere with this suitcase on wheels. I assume it operates as his portable office, rather than a percussion instrument. The dogs bark at Dave again, as usual, but soon settle down. Dotty wants to sit on my lap while we have our meetings. After all these years I suppose I still find it a little invasive that so many meetings are held in our home. I guess that's one of the many sacrifices you make when you foster – frequently having people inside your house who you would probably never choose to spend time with in any other walk of life.

Dave makes himself comfortable in our kitchen – a place he has been visiting regularly for several months now, ever since he took over as our supervising social worker. He always sits in the same spot, and although I'm used to the sight of him spreading over the kitchen chair, he always seems just slightly too large for the room.

Overall, Dave is rated by most people I know as a good social worker. He does not like to rock the boat, he tries to keep everyone placid, and he is always keen to 'manage expectations'. For me, this is not necessarily my preferred way of approaching things. Perhaps if I was working with, I don't know, bricks, or kettles, or even rose bushes, I might be of the same mind, but when you have children and young people, often in trauma, to look after, waiting is not something I want to do. The whole system has become one giant, fat, ugly, lumpy, slow behemoth of a bureaucratic experiment gone wrong. Everyone within it moans about it, but I have, so far, never found anyone who has suggested, let alone created, anything else. It simply does not work at the speed needed to react to the crisis in these children's lives.

And recently, Lloyd and I have both begun to feel that Dave is 'managing' us in very careful ways. We have been fobbed off a few times, and not told everything that we might need to hear. Having worked in the corporate world for years, Lloyd is much better at dealing with this side of things than I am. When I feel like screaming and my inner (traumatised) child wants to kick up the dust, he is calm and patient and rational – though I know that he feels the same things as I do. He is simply much better at handling it.

This morning I follow his lead, and we politely sit there for the best part of an hour while we 'suck it up' and listen to what Dave has to say.

Lloyd has assured me that it's just easier this way. 'Let them do what they have to do, and say what they have to say.'

Until we start to talk directly about Stella and Debbie, and I sense something quite different about Dave's manner and mood.

'Right, so then,' he pauses. 'I have been chasing Debbie, as you know, but she is *still* on sick leave.' To my surprise, he runs his fingers through his hair as he emphasises the 'still', which makes me notice that he seems to be growing it a little longer than the close crop he has generally sported in the past. Then he follows this information up with a rare but pointed comment on the situation. 'Yes. It would have been more helpful if we had known this when we were forced to make certain decisions.'

Dave is traditional in his approach. Lloyd stops me whenever I try to describe him as 'old school', but actually this is the bit that I really like about him. He does things thoroughly. He reads and answers his emails in a timely way, and almost always responds immediately to telephone calls. I appreciate this, especially given the frustrations I have felt in trying to get hold of Debbie of late. Dave is an i-dotter and a t-crosser, and while I am not, always, I understand the importance of it in the work that he does. He documents our meetings faithfully, is never critical of the system, never says anything 'off the record' and generally toes the party line with measured pragmatism, if not enthusiasm. Though I warm to someone like WPC Julie Watters, who seems prepared to bend the rules now and then to achieve the desired results, I also respect Dave for his precise and careful handling of all our dealings.

He goes on, 'Consequently, I have informed Debbie's manager that, for now, and for the foreseeable future, Stella will not be attending any contact visits due to the nature of the disclosures and ongoing investigations by the police.'

He says all of this without me having to prompt the issue in any way, and my heart does a little leap. I am surprised by the directness of his 'I have informed,' because he is usually more passive than this, not given to declaratives. I realise that Julie must have been in contact with Dave, and probably with Debbie's manager, too. Good on her. She is a persuasive influence, the WPC.

'So, there is a meeting of all the various professionals scheduled for next week to discuss Stella's situation,' Dave explains.

I ask who will be there.

'Debbie is evidently out for a while longer yet, I don't know the exact details – and so a locum will be covering for her. She's looking through Stella's file this week in order to get up to speed.'

My heart sinks a little. I know better than anyone that 'looking through the file' is not going to get anyone 'up to speed' in a case like this. I spent a long time looking at the file myself when Stella first arrived. It doesn't have all the answers. And now there is to be another professional getting involved, starting from a position of no knowledge once more. There just doesn't seem to be any kind of continuity for this poor child. Dave acknowledges my raised eyebrow with one of his own, and continues.

'Debbie's manager will be there, as well as WPC Watters and another colleague of hers from the police force. Stella's teacher, Mrs Griffiths, is likely to attend if they will let her out of school – you know her – and with her maybe the SENCO worker. The IRO will be present and, of course, me and you two.'

The accepted abbreviations always take me a while to process, even though I have been in this game for many years now. The IRO is the Independent Reviewing Officer, and the SENCO is the Special Educational Needs Coordinator from the school. I ask if anyone from a therapeutic occupation will be there. Dave looks at me, pointedly, and says, 'Cutbacks.'

It is almost as if he is throwing it out there as a challenge. When he doesn't get the response he knows I might usually give to this, (I'm sitting on my hands and trying to heed all of Lloyd's advice – a rant isn't going to help in this moment) he goes a little further than he usually does.

'Money shouldn't have to be an issue for a child in this situation. I know that and you know that. But now it's all about the money. There simply isn't any.'

I'm momentarily floored by this admission, and so Dave, who I would ordinarily describe as pretty buttoned-up, sees his moment to plough ahead.

'I don't know if you will have heard the full details of this yet, but all the family support services have been axed. They are cutting contact workers, so carers will have to step up and fill that role.'

I lower my eyebrows and feel the deep crease form at the centre of my forehead. I have no words.

Then in an even more surprisingly candid revelation, Dave says, 'I've had enough. The whole thing's untenable.' He doesn't look me in the eye but stares across the kitchen. 'So…' This time the pause is longer before his final revelation. 'I'm packing it in. My wife and I are opening up a florist together.'

Lloyd and I sit there with our thoughts in a tailspin. Sometimes the world of fostering can feel like it's falling apart, and, in the midst of all of this are the children: the vulnerable, traumatised children.

Dave's parting shot is to tell us that he has given notice and has just three months before he leaves. He assures us that he will do everything he can to support us in the meantime – and Stella. I know that he means it, and although I am pleased to hear it, I wonder if he will be as painstaking as he has always been in the past through the final weeks of his employment in social services. My feelings are also tempered by the knowledge that we will now have to go through the whole process of meeting and getting to know another supervising social worker. You just never know what they are going to be like, or if we will be able to get on with them. Relationships take a long time to build. I cuddle Dotty a little tighter into my arms. There are rocky times ahead.

Chapter 11

Lily and Stella stroll past the window holding onto the handles at either end of a large, transparent plastic box. Their treasure chest is structured into little compartments, each filled with dozens of tiny elastic bands grouped in colours. In the other, free hand, each child carries a selection of the little hooks and tools required to perform the tiny darting movements that will turn the bands into friendship bracelets and key rings. Loom bands seem to have had an unexpected resurgence. I've noticed over the last few days varying lengths of the woven bands in two and three-way colour combinations snaking their way into various corners of the house. I smile to myself. Picking up discarded bands, though irritating, is easier than extracting glittering, glutinous slime globules from the fringes of rugs. Could it be that slime has had its day for the time being? If so, I'm happy for the latest craze.

I am in my studio, working on illustration number six in the series. The branches of the background trees are becoming increasingly tangled up and menacing shapes seem to have taken up residence in the interstices of the middle ground. The prettily plumaged bird that I had mentally sketched is not willing to make his, or perhaps her, appearance and I know that Stella is making her presence felt in my painting once again.

One of the unnerving things about Stella – alongside those large, beseeching eyes – is her calm and her stillness with her quiet. There is none of the rambunctiousness of the average five-year-old, clumsily feeling their way to honing fine and gross motor skills. Stella is entirely self-contained: a neat little package of a person, who would easily meet the demands of the Victorian convention for children to be seen and not heard. Her natural timidity means that she carries herself carefully and gracefully with a peculiarly adult poise. She barely speaks, never initiates dialogue, only ever responds. When she does talk it is with an extreme level of politeness, and reminds me of the little underwater popping sounds of a guppy or an angel fish. Singing along to her favourite songs in the car she is mostly just mouthing the words, though a little, involuntary sound might just escape now and then.

She communicates mostly with those expressive eyes, disturbingly deep-sunk into their sockets, thereby giving the impression that they are too large, too wide, and too wide open for her delicate face. Outside Yad Vashem, the world Holocaust remembrance centre in Jerusalem, there is a statue of the biblical Ruth, crying out to God to save the children. The sculptor has chosen to depict that tortured entreaty by turning Ruth's whole face into one black hole. Her screaming mouth *is* her head. For Stella, her entire head seems to consist of those soulful orbs that we know now must have seen far, far too much in her short little life.

So, when she finally uses her voice and I hear the shouting, I come running. I drop everything in the studio when the terrible sound comes. Dark green paint from my brush puddles on the floor.

The words that come from Stella's mouth are as shocking as they are unexpected. They are screeched at the top of a voice range that we simply didn't know she possessed. And, my goodness, do they resound loud and clear.

'You fucking cunting twat!'

Lily has dropped Stella's containers of elastic bands onto the floor. They are pooled in little coloured molehills on the floorboards when I arrive on the scene.

'It was an accident!' Lily looks at me in shock, and jumps down automatically on all fours, scrabbling to start picking up the bands, to clear the mess. Despite all her own earlier life trauma, swearing has never really been her thing. And although the little coloured elastics are everywhere, this is not a 'mess' that Lily has created. Not 20 seconds ago they were laughing and purposeful and happy, about to embark on their next creative project. Although Lily will understand on some fundamental level later that she is not responsible for it – indeed perhaps understands right in this moment – it is still very difficult to have this abusive language directed at you.

I shoo Lily out of the room and bend down slowly to carry on collecting up the stray bands. Stella is beside herself, shaking with anger. I let her carry on with whatever she needs to do.

'Fucking cunt!'

Then, 'You fucking arsehole.'

Next, 'You wait! I will fucking stick my fist so far up your cunt it will knock your eyes out.'

It goes on and on. It's like a scene from *Fight Club*, but with worse language. I keep a mental record of everything she says. I'm not easily shocked, but hearing this torrent of filth spewing from the mouth of a tiny person is more than unpleasant. It shakes me to the core.

I am onto the purple elastic bands now and the steady picking up helps me to rationalise what she might be feeling now that she feels safer and does not have to go back to contact. This is a release, of sorts, for her.

She stands there wringing her hands while the effing and jeffing continues. I no longer recognise the puckered, angry face from which these words are all spewing. Even the actions in her tiny body seem to belong to another being. Lloyd is standing by the kitchen door by now. He is as appalled as I am. He manages to display nothing more than his disappointed-dad face. He loves his girls, all of them, the big ones who have left home and our little ones living here now.

Under other circumstances, this scene might be funny. My darker sense of humour – that I blame entirely on early childhood trauma (it can come in handy sometimes) – does indeed begin to find the spectacle mildly amusing. Stella looks like a willowy pre-Raphaelite beauty but sounds, right now, like a drunken docker.

And I know that this really isn't funny at all. I have heard many children swear because they heard their parents swear. Indeed, my old neighbours (who were both successful architects) had a little boy the same age as Jackson. I was looking after the boys one day when they must have been about four, and as we were driving along the road behind a rubbish collection lorry, the little boy piped up, with all the intonation of his middle-class parents, 'Those fucking bins.' I remember hiding a smile and knowing that he hadn't a clue what he was saying.

Lloyd ushers everyone else away from the room very gently and efficiently. The boys are well used to it. Though they too came running at the first expletive, they're not frightened or even much alarmed: they understand that our foster children have not experienced the charmed and stable lives they have. They get it, and always want to know how to help, whichever foster child it has been in the past – and Stella has become very special to us.

What I do find deeply troubling is the explicit and graphic nature of Stella's outburst. *I will fucking stick my fist so far up your cunt it will knock your eyes out* is not something that has been overheard in the playground. As soon as I am able to move out of this scenario I will let Julie know exactly what Stella has said.

There's no such thing as the perfect foster carer. And if there is, I am far from it, but I have to do something in this moment. Stella is still shouting and swearing when I gently move towards her. The elastic bands are all back in their box now. I carefully rest my hands on her wrists and look straight into her face, into those big eyes, pupils dilated to unnatural proportions, giant in those already too-large pools. In a soothing, sing-song voice, as though nothing at all is out of the ordinary, I say, 'Stella would you like a hot chocolate and a cookie?'

She looks straight back at me and the composed, polite, elfin figure that we recognise returns. In a fraction of a second, the demons have vanished. She is almost surprised as she looks around her.

She nods slowly and says, meekly, 'Yes please, Louise.' All the decibels are gone from the volume in her voice again.

I mention nothing, make no reference to what has just happened. I don't cross-examine her. I don't know what else to do but simply let her be. She stays very close to me while I move around the kitchen assembling milk, cookies, mugs and plates – the accoutrements of a civilised break. I set it all out at the end of the kitchen table and sit down. I hold out my arms and smile, 'Fancy a hug, Stella?'

I hope that she feels safe again now, and know that this has probably made her very, very tired. Up she gets and nestles right into me. She rocks herself to sleep in my arms while the drink goes cold and the biscuit is not eaten.

Lloyd pokes his head around the door and indicates that he has made a bed up on the sofa. Lily is standing next to him, her face full of concern. She knows, too. We have had plenty of unexpected moments with outbursts from Lily – though not the expletives, to be sure. They always provoke the same response in me: simply, 'What did they do to you?'

I ask Lily to go and get Stella's duvet and teddy, which she does in a flash without a blink or murmur. I settle Stella's light body on the sofa. There really is nothing of her. It seems impossible that the string of invectives came with such venom from this gentle creature just a few minutes before. Lily is back in a flash and helps me to cover her up. She pats the duvet down gently and places Stella's teddy into her arms. I fiddle around and find something gentle and nondescript on the television. An afternoon drama that isn't very dramatic. Voices and music that are reassuring and soothing.

We leave her to her uneasy sleep.

Chapter 12

I do everything I can to simply slow the world down for Stella in the aftermath of her outburst. I calm our ordinary family chaos as much as I can, avoid calling out, making loud noises or any surprises in our routine. The other children understand implicitly. Stella's little head and her heart need some rest. It is not that the atmosphere is subdued – far from it. It is more that a heightened calm settles over us all and blankets the household.

A perhaps not unexpected side-effect of Stella's 'moment' (one of a number of euphemistic phrases that we are using to refer to it) is that she is unusually clingy for the next few days. For the rest of the weekend she wants me to hold her, to reassure her, and I am happy to oblige – to be able to do anything to help her get through this. She doesn't seem to want to be left on her own at all, doesn't let me out of her sight if she can possibly help it, and that excessive level of politeness which always characterised her speech has resumed.

There is no sign of that incredible rage, or any hint that any of that violent and sexualised language might resurface. It feels to me as though she has purged a great deal of pain, anger and fear through her explosion. Perhaps it is a kind of exorcism. And yet, experience has taught me that there is likely to be more to come. Something has been unleashed in Stella and it may not be able to stop. It's as if a kettle reached boiling point and steam erupted from the whistling spout – the lid is back on for now, and that steam will take a long time to cool. But it will only take a little bit of heat reapplied for another explosive outburst.

I have experienced many eruptions of behaviour like Stella's, and so on one level it does not faze us too badly as a family this time. But I do watch the others carefully, to be sure. There can sometimes be a backlash from the other children. After an event like this Lily has been known to have a little ripple of her own, perhaps a scaled-down imitation of what happened as if she needs to try it out for herself, while the boys tend to be a little livelier, as though they want attention too.

It has only become a real problem in the past when a child has attacked one of them physically. That is hard. That is when you question whether fostering is a good idea. Thankfully this has not happened very often, and now that they are older and bigger I think it will become less of an issue.

Memories resurface for me. I have my own first-hand experience of a Stella-style outburst. In fact, I remember having a few of these 'sessions' myself. One happened when

I was a few years older than Stella. I would have been about 11. Barbara, my adopted mother, was messing with my head – as was her way. She had spent years systematically destroying any self-confidence I might have mustered, by constructing a world in which I could do no right. Everything I said was wrong, each word that came from my mouth a manifestation of my worthlessness. Everything I did was criticised and mocked. She created the circumstances in which I knew that I was intrinsically bad, and this was reinforced with every single action I took. Believing it as an absolute truth of my existence, I became the 'bad' that she repeatedly told me I was. On this particular day, I finally gave myself over to the unspeakable emotions that were overwhelming me, and I ceased to have any meaningful control over my reactions. I tipped bins over, pulled a climbing plant clean off the wall, upended garden chairs, kicked the standing spade and other metal tools so that they clattered and fell like dominoes. I stood then, in the middle of the garden, surveyed my destruction and screamed and screamed like a banshee until it felt as though the blood would burst through my veins and give me the release I needed from the constant condemnation, fault-finding and denunciation.

And so I understand something about Stella and what has happened to her. I was not being naughty, and neither was she. My mind and body had gone beyond the level of abuse that it could tolerate and needed to vent. Barbara actually called the police that day, though they went away again without intervening in any meaningful way. To any outsider I was just an out-of-control child having a tantrum. Getting the police involved simply piled on the truth of my absolute knowledge about the 'wrongness' of my existence.

We actually have someone in the village who has unhelpfully called the police a few times while our foster children have been having their 'venting occasions'. He's not one of my favourite people in the community, as might be imagined. And it's not just for the lack of understanding in getting the police involved. Once I managed to accidentally get myself stuck in a conversation with him and another local out in the street while walking the dog, just at the time that the Jimmy Savile case was at its peak. New and horrific revelations of his misdemeanours were splashed across the front pages each day, and pouring constantly out of every radio and television set.

He said, 'I've had enough of it. I wish they would all just shut up about bloody child abuse. Honestly. It happened years ago. Why can't they all just get over it?'

Bloody child abuse? Just get over it? I used up my quota of expletives when I shared some of Stella's on the previous pages, so I won't go there again. It can be left to the imagination what I think of him.

Thankfully no one called the police while Stella was having her 'time' (another euphemism – I have plenty more). He was something of a lone voice in our community. All of our other neighbours are wonderful, and generally very supportive – especially when they learn about my own childhood and background and what we are trying to do for the children who come to us.

Sunday morning comes. Stella sits at the table while I prepare lunch. She has my big pot of drawing pencils next to her and a new sketchbook, white pages as yet unblemished. While I was peeling the potatoes just now she had been threading a necklace. A few moments before this, I sat and talked about my own family. When a foster child realises that I am like them and that I can relate to their experience, something is likely to happen. It can be both good and bad. I have met many dysfunctional, but more often perfectly functional adults who grew up in care and have experienced childhood abuse. I find it wonderful and fascinating that we are not the self-fulfilling prophecies that some who worked with us had predicted – often quite the opposite.

I told Stella that I had never met my dad and that there had been some adults in my life when I was a child who I had no choice but to depend upon and believe in. I explained how they hurt me and made me feel sad and lonely. Now I have my back to her as, potatoes now peeled, I chop them into good roasting sizes on the chopping board and add them to the pan. Behind me, she has put the necklace down and I can hear the sound of fast drawing, pencils on paper.

When I turn round again, she has gone back to threading the necklace but the sketchbook is closed and positioned towards my end of the table. It's as though she is inviting me to open it, placed forward as if to say, 'please look'.

I gesture towards it. There is an almost imperceptible inclination of her head towards the book.

Standing at the end of the kitchen table, I open the page and see a picture of a man – I think it is a man – and a much smaller person with long hair which I take to be Stella. I am struck by the little person's sad face and the fact that she has no arms. The adult has arms and he is smiling but she is sad, and helpless. I see enough to make me want to sit down and turn the next page.

Again there is a small person, who must be Stella, standing between two big people. One is a man, the other is a woman. Just as before, the small person has a big red down-turned mouth, no smile then – and this time, tears. The adults are smiling. The man has big spiky teeth, like a shark. His arm, which looks like a rounders bat in her drawing, is reaching down towards her genital area. The woman is smiling and smoking. I feel terrible. As I look up to Stella she quickly moves her eyes – that have been on me – back to threading her beads. I turn the page again. Oh no. This time there are three men, with similar spiky hair, but this is not their most distinguishing feature. All three have big erect penises. The faces are each smiling again, with disproportionately big teeth. One of the men has been given giant *red* teeth. I feel horrid. I put the book down. I feel her shame. Three of them. I hope that this is not an accurate depiction of a single moment. I don't know what I hope. There is nothing much good to 'hope' from an image like this. I pick it up again, so that she knows that I am not rejecting it. I get up and walk round the table.

I crouch down beside her with the book in my hands and say, 'Thank you, Stella. Thank you for being so brave.'

How vulnerable and exposed we feel when we share something of ourselves in drawing, or writing, or indeed any art form.

She makes a little movement with her mouth and carries on making the necklace.

Of course, I know that art can often be a way for children to articulate things that they might otherwise be unable to express, to tell stories that would be left unsaid because the words didn't exist, but the medium of the image is often exploratory and frequently symbolic or expressionistic. It has been a long time since I have seen anything as stark and horribly explicit as the narrative that leaps from these pages. It is a gallery of abuse and, more than that, it is a physical expression of Stella's recognition, or perception, of her utter helplessness in those moments, in those scenes. I am reeling. Whether it is indeed an accurate, literal depiction of something that happened as a one-off, or worse, repeatedly, or even if it is a less literal representation of what has happened to her, it is terrible. Surprisingly, it isn't the engorged penises that burn into my brain. It is the giant shark teeth of all the adults that remain etched into my skull.

By the time Sunday afternoon comes around I feel that a trip to the park might be in order. Fresh air and a change of scene will do us all good. After the warmth of the last few days, there are colder currents on the air. I dash back to the house for my cardigan and force Lily and Stella to take light jackets with them. I see that Lily is about to protest at the perceived invasion of her civil liberties and curtailment of her freedom of choice. Her mouth opens to debate the requirement, but she thinks better of it and takes the proffered jacket with a nod. Stella, of course, accepts hers compliantly.

Even though autumn should not be with us just yet, large pine cones litter the path into the park. They are in various states of disintegration and decay and lie drunkenly in piles of dried-out orange pine needles that have worked their way into every groove and crack and crevice of the path. Stella aims delicate, shuffling kicks at them, rolling them onto the grass and clearing the path. We have brought bikes and scooters with us so that they can ride up and down on them. If only it was easy to kick all the obstacles out of Stella's path. Somehow it feels as if summer is over before it has even begun.

Monday morning arrives far too quickly, before any of us, especially Stella, are ready.

After the school run I get busy with my emails, carefully wording my logs so that Stella will, at some point in her future, have some positive information that will enable her to understand how her trauma played out. I construct a narrative that doesn't diminish from the seriousness of the episode, but emphasises that she was right, and more than entitled to have her 'moment', her outburst – as well as any more that may come. I take copies of her artwork, which speaks for itself and doesn't need any of my deconstructive analysis to make sense of it.

An Egress email pings into my inbox. It's from Trudy Brown, the locum and temporary replacement for Debbie. She has scheduled the professionals' meeting to talk about Stella for Thursday morning at 10am. Into the diary it goes.

Next, I call Dave and leave a quick message to say that I would like to have a catch-up before Thursday. I want to know his views on the latest development and want him to hear it from me directly as well as reading about it in a log. Now that he is feeling 'demob' happy there is a chance that his candid manner from last week might continue. I'm hoping that he will be more open and actually say something instead of his usual sitting on the fence – after all, he's made it quite clear that he does not want to continue as a social worker, so he has nothing to lose.

Dave calls me back within half an hour. Yes, I can detect a definite lightness in his voice. I don't blame him. He can clearly see the light at the end of the tunnel. I explain about Stella's moment and he is supportive. He seems genuinely concerned. He acknowledges our former experience in dealing with things like this, and that he is sure we went about things the right way and made her feel safe.

Dave is well aware that we once looked after a young girl who tried to kill herself, and very nearly succeeded. It's why the lock, in a bathroom where a succession of traumatised children have bathed, needs to be not too tightly screwed in. Tricks of the trade in being able to gain access in an emergency.

As our supervising social worker, at least for the time being, he has met Stella and been enchanted by her in the way that all of us have. She is one of those children that find themselves a little place in a good person's heart.

We go on to talk about the meeting. Dave thinks they will want to discuss the plan that the locum has devised in Debbie's absence. I take a deep breath and say once again what I have heard myself say many times before this. 'But she hasn't even met Stella.'

Dave makes an 'mmmmh' sound in agreement.

'How can she make any sort of a plan without having even met her?' I spit the word 'plan' out.

The soothing noises continue on the other end of the phone.

It has not been discussed exactly how long we are looking after Stella for. There have been times in the past where I have had the sense that if the emergency placement is working then the authorities leave the child alone and run on to the next crisis. We have all become deeply fond of Stella and that tug of attachment is there. I feel a sense of threat towards us because a social worker that none of us have ever met, and that we know nothing about, is making plans for a troubled little girl who we have all fallen in love with.

I can't bring myself to raise the issue with Dave. He tells me to 'hang in there, Louise,' and we hang up. I sit with the phone in my hand for a long time, staring at it and wondering what power I have to change the course of what is about to happen.

Lloyd and I have learned that logic is not always the main factor in the thinking of the 'corporate parent.' In some ways we have to protect ourselves as much as Stella, and we also know that the plan has to be what's best for Stella. This takes on a slightly different twist when you are fully aware that there is no money left in the system – and your decision makers are in special measures with Ofsted.

It's a hard one to try to balance in your own mind, because at the end of the day, no matter how hard we advocate, or even Dave advocates, for Stella, the corporate parent will do what it wants anyway.

My main concern is the lack of knowledge in this case, not just from a locum social worker who knows nothing of the recent history, but all the way through. How much information was missing from the file at the start, how much WPC Julie Watters and I have uncovered about the trauma that Stella has clearly suffered. I haven't met the Independent Reviewing Officer. In fact, I know even less about the IRO than I do about the locum. At least I have her name.

In the early days of our fostering, Lloyd used to say, 'Don't rock the boat, Louise.' He doesn't say that anymore.

We find our voices being lost in the clamour, or rejected entirely, when we are precisely the ones who know the child better than the state and all the agencies can possibly hope to.

It's a hard path to walk, a bitter pill to swallow, a hard circle to square, and any other cliche that you care to mention. The answer to that question of how much power we have?

Precisely none.

Chapter 13

It's Thursday, and 10am looms large. The meeting day has arrived. I choose my outfit carefully: a smart dress in bright colours matched with a tailored, collarless jacket. They will notice me today, I tell my reflection in the mirror as I straighten the hemline. I say goodbye to the children and leave a little earlier than usual to get Stella to school and me into town in time to find a decent parking space and arrive in a timely fashion at the social services building.

In the days and hours before, and right at the start of a meeting like this, I say to myself, 'Stay calm, Louise. Be the better person. Be professional.' It is a little mantra that I find myself repeating sometimes during the meeting.

Lloyd can't come to this one. He's cross because he really wants to be there, and I could do with the emotional support that his presence would bring. On this occasion his graphic design duties have called him to a two-day meeting away from home, and there is nothing that he can do about the timing of it.

His meetings, as I understand it, frequently end up at the bar and then a restaurant —and generally everyone wants the same outcome. The professionals' meetings for a 'Looked After Child', an LAC, sometimes even turned into a noun and pronounced as 'lac', are not like that at all. Managers have one eye on the budget, and this case is complicated by several other factors. A new social worker may want to mark her territory. Dave, because of his imminent departure, may not want a fight. The IRO, who is really in the dark having never met Stella, needs to Chair the meeting and communicate that they have read everything. And waiting on the other side of the table, there's me. What are my 'complications'? I am a seasoned foster carer with lots of confidence.

As I walk into the reception area I give myself another quick recital of 'Stay calm, Louise. Be the better person. Be professional.' I stand behind a tall man in a black suit and hear him say that he's here for the 10am meeting with Trudy Brown. He signs in. There is a tap on my shoulder. I turn around and see the lovely WPC Julie Watters.

She points to the man in the suit and says, in the best tradition of television crime

dramas, 'Louise, I've brought back-up.'

Back-up, it transpires, is Sergeant Nick Daniels. He shakes my hand, and even though I am 'being professional', I am struck by his loveliness. Smiley blue eyes sit below a floppy fringe of flaxen hair. He is a cross between a young Robert Redford and Tom Hiddleston, and even though I have two decades on him and am happily married, I find myself straightening my skirt and patting my hair down when he isn't looking, and laughing slightly too loudly at his jokes when he is. Mantra time again.

Julie has a folder in her hand and brandishes it in a manner that suggests she is not afraid to use it. We sit down together on the seats in the reception area. Julie asks how Stella has been, and I fill her in about the weekend's outburst and Stella's behaviour since, just as Dave walks in. He works in a building only a block away, so is without a coat. He just carries his notebook and pen and his badge. I introduce Nick and Julie to Dave.

Dave smiles, 'We've met. I've worked with Nick before.' Lucky him.

'That's helpful then,' Julie chips in. 'You'll realise the gravity of this case.'

'I am beginning to.'

I sit quietly, taking in those words that destroy all of my momentary flippancy. What do they mean? Nick must have a very particular role within the police force. I shiver. What has happened to Stella?

There is a pause. A reception area is not the place to discuss what is clearly taking on a more serious tenor than even I had realised. Nick moves to the window and whistles to himself, lifting the mood somewhat. Julie smiles at me reassuringly. Time passes. It's 10.15, a quarter of an hour past the allotted meeting time, and no one has been down to get us. Nick looks at his watch and rolls his eyes. We chat about this and that to while away the time. I even join in with a conversation about football, a subject that I know nothing about. And when I say nothing, I mean nothing. Lloyd still thinks it's hilarious that I thought Pele was Italian.

We begin to lower our heads and our voices as Julie says, 'It's been half an hour now. A few minutes, fair enough, but half an hour late? What do they think they're playing at?'

Dave shakes his head in a non-committal way. Nick fiddles with his watch and rearranges his long, crossed legs. The hands on the clock above the reception desk continue to tick round. I suggest that I ask the receptionist if they can try calling Trudy again. My colleagues – and I do feel that we are 'in league' now – think that this is a good idea. I stand by the desk as the apologetic man puts a call through to Trudy's number. I can't hear the conversation but can guess what is communicated by the throat-clearing 'I see' and 'mmm, okay' sounds he makes. He puts the phone down and looks at me a little sheepishly.

'I'm sorry. Trudy and her manger are running late. They aren't sure how much longer they will be. They send their apologies for keeping you waiting.' It's not his fault, but I can only manage a tight smile in return as I thank him for trying.

The hands on the clock have now crept round to 10.45. The morning is disappearing. None of us are impressed. Nick stands up and walks around a bit. He mutters under his breath, 'They're not the only ones with work to do.'

Julie is looking decidedly nonplussed. I'm starting to feel a little bit annoyed now. I am booked in to talk to my agent at 1pm. I strongly suspect that I'm not going to make it at this rate, and I know that she's super busy. She's negotiating a new book deal for me. I quietly wonder how people like Trudy would cope in a job like Julie's or Nick's.

It is after 11.15am and several more conversations with the unfortunate gentleman on reception later, when the door behind reception finally opens and two people enter the room.

The first is a young woman with long, dark, straightened hair that is impossibly glossy. She is dressed in a tight black top and pale-blue skinny jeans over silver Converse All Star shoes. Next to her is a skinny, grey-haired man, his hair is styled into a rockabilly quiff, and his flowery shirt reminds me of something that the presenters from Top Gear might wear. His jeans are ripped at the knee. Both are casually carrying coffee cups. Large, ostentatious disposable coffee cups brought in from a coffee house chain, the brand shouting itself out from the plastic sides. I can't help but wonder if a dash from the office to a coffee shop has been part of what has kept us waiting for so long.

I can feel Nick and Julie's anger rising beside mine.

'Is it dress-down Thursday?' Nick enquires.

I find myself stifling a giggle, in spite of the gravity of the nature of this meeting.

Silver Converse says 'No,' in a tone that reveals that she has completely missed Nick's point, before introducing herself as Trudy without either a smile or handshake.

We follow them up several flights of stairs. They lead, but neither turns around at any point to check that we are keeping up. There is no small talk. No conversation at all. They look more like art lecturers than social care professionals. Even I, with my flair for arty, unconventional sartorial choices have made much more of an effort to look smart. It feels like a slight of sorts, a little dig at us, somehow.

There is no sign of Stella's teacher, or of the SENCO, so there is no support from that corner. Thus far, it is feeling very adversarial.

We enter a room with an olive-shaped table and blue chairs. It is stuffy and stinks of perspiration and other unpleasant odours that suggest the recent proximity of human bodies. I ask if we can open the window. The grey-haired skinny man, who has not yet introduced himself, walks to the window and looks at the fixings.

'No. I don't think we can.'

That is not good enough for Nick, who walks over to where Rockabilly Quiff is standing, reaches across the glass to the frame, lifts a handle, presses something and pushes open the window. He gives me a wry smile and sits down. Is there an equivalent of the Richter Scale to measure tension? If so, we could do with it.

Rockabilly Quiff, it turns out, is actually Tony, the IRO who looks like he is going to chair the meeting today. I look at his and Trudy's coffee cups and somehow know that they will not be offering us refreshments. Dave pulls a bottle of water out from under his file. I didn't see that earlier. He definitely knows how these meetings are run.

Tony asks if we can go round the room and introduce ourselves.

Trudy starts, 'Trudy, child social worker.' Still no nicety, all formality – so at odds with the impression the coffee cups and clothes give.

'Tony, IRO. I will be chairing the meeting today.'

Nick follows their lead. 'Sergeant Nick Daniels. CID.'

'WPC Julie Watters, police child protection.'

Then me. 'Louise Allen. Foster Carer.' I feel as though I am introducing myself in front of Jeremy Paxman on *University Challenge*. I just hope no one asks me what my degree is in.

Trudy has a pile of paperwork in front of her, but her first question makes me wonder if she has read it. 'Stella's surname?'

It seems as though we are dispensing with grammatical constructions entirely. So I say only, 'Artois-Bennett.'

Trudy looks at her notes. 'Is she French?'

I look at Nick across the table. He has a very good deadpan face, but even having only met him this morning, I know that he will be thinking all kinds of things that may not be entirely appropriate in a professional context. He is a consummate professional, though, and gives nothing away.

I cough. 'No, she's not French, no.'

There is an awkward pause and I feel the need to fill it. 'Stella was actually named after the drink – Stella Artois.'

Tony laughs. 'Wow! Well, that's original.'

There is another awkward pause, because I don't share his laughter.

'Right, then.' Tony clears his throat, looks at Nick and asks if he can bring us up to speed.

Nick looks straight back at Tony and says, 'Actually, WPC Watters is the reporting officer who interviewed Stella.'

I have the impression that Tony is the kind of man who will only accept the authority of another man. Julie's file is already open, her notes are clearly laid out, her pen is ready, and she begins. Julie talks about her first visit to our house where she met me and my family and Stella. It seems such a long time ago, but it is actually only a few short weeks. She reports that the atmosphere in our home was 'relaxed and happy'.

Aww, that's nice, I think to myself.

'Louise had already raised a number of concerns at this point, as you will be aware.'

Both Trudy and Tony rifle through their notes. Their behaviour suggests that they were very much not aware.

Julie, who has no need to refer to her notes, continues, 'While playing happily in the garden with Louise's other foster child and two of her friends, and Louise's two birth sons, Louise and her husband, Lloyd, gathered the children together to take a photograph. As Lloyd and Louise called out 'say cheese' to make the children smile, Stella dropped to the floor, removed her underwear, laid on her back, raised her legs and parted them so that her genital area was directed towards the camera.'

This is such a horrible story that still makes me shudder when it is related, even in such a detached and clinical way. Nevertheless, I begin to feel as though I am in some sort of farce when Tony says,

'Can you be absolutely sure that this is sexually related behaviour?'

I look at Nick. His face is still deadpan, but its features are darkening.

Julie, ever pragmatic, intervenes. 'Well, perhaps not, Tony, on its own. But as you will have seen from the file, there have been a cluster of other incidents that, taken together, absolutely suggest that Stella has been sexually coerced and abused.

Now it is Trudy's turn to direct a question. 'And, so, WPC…' she breaks off to check the name, 'Watters, do you intend for Stella to have a hospital medical investigation?'

Julie is very calm. 'No, Trudy, we don't. Not at this time.'

She's good at this name thing.

'Because, Trudy, whatever happened was clearly a while ago now. There will not be any medical evidence that we can use at this stage in the investigation. But for her future health, at some stage Stella may need a full medical to ensure that her vagina – and other areas – are okay.'

She is FIVE! I want to scream. JUST FIVE YEARS OLD! What kind of hellish world do we live in where a young child should need a vaginal examination? But I don't say anything, of course. I just feel sad.

Julie goes on to say that their investigations have led them to believe that both Shannon and Terry, Stella's dad, had abused Stella or been complicit in her abuse. 'Terry is currently serving an eight-year prison sentence. At this moment we are unable to locate Shannon. Apparently, after the last contact visit, she has…' Here she pauses for a fraction. '…moved on.' She raises her eyes as if to invite discussion of the decision to resume contact. It is a challenge to Trudy, and to Tony, although in fairness to them, it was not their decision, personally. They have some important decisions to make now, though.

And Julie's words make me think long and hard about the now-missing Shannon. I remember clocking her through the round window in the red double doors at the family centre. I remember the way that our eyes locked – foster carer and birth mother. Both like fierce tigresses. Perhaps she looked at me and realised that I knew something was wrong. Would a few seconds be enough for her to tell that I was like a dog with a bone? That I would just keep going at it, never giving up, until I got the answer. I wonder if I have been instrumental in sending her on the run.

Nick steps in to hammer the point home. 'We are widening our search for Shannon and although at this stage we only want to bring her in for questioning, it is in relation to a *criminal* investigation.' He allows that to sink in before continuing, 'The descriptions of Stella's behaviour, and the comments that she herself has made, bear some striking hallmarks that are consistent with a number of other cases. These cases stretch across three cities and their surrounding towns. I don't think I need to say any more about the potential seriousness of this. We are talking about a highly organised, systematic paedophile ring.'

Trudy and Tony are quiet now. I wonder how many other children are involved and have now got to spend the rest of their lives working this out.

There is a long, awkward pause in the still stuffy room.

'Will Stella receive any support?' I ask.

'Ye-es,' says Trudy, and I already don't like the way that she has broken that word into two syllables. She thumbs through her paperwork. 'We are looking at the Future Journeys programme for her.'

I have heard of it. American, expensive, and only 12 weeks long.

'Would that be it, or would that be part of a broader and longer plan?' I ask. Now that their uncomfortable questions are over, and the power and perhaps the agenda in the room seem to have shifted somewhat, I feel that I can offer some of my own, uncomfortable questions.

Trudy says, 'We feel at this stage that Stella would benefit from this programme. It has had some excellent results.'

I don't know how a newish programme like this one – and I follow developments in the field avidly – could create data to demonstrate that it is successful. The old teacher in me can't leave it. 'And what do "excellent results" look like to you, Trudy?' I tag on her name like Julie has been doing.

Trudy flicks her hair and leans forward. 'CSE children have settled much faster after being on this programme.'

Another abbreviation to mitigate a terrible reality: CSE is shorthand for Child Sexual Exploitation. This isn't a general child. This is Stella. 'Are we on a time schedule here, Trudy? Surely it takes as long as it takes with good support – and much longer or never without the right support.'

I know what this is about: funding again. A new company has come along offering a cheaper package, and therefore that is what Stella will get. A cheaper, second-rate, not quite good enough service. The voice inside me screams. Outwardly I am still calm, although I can't keep the scathing tone from my voice. This makes me so cross.

'How can you put a *cost* on a child recovering from what we believe has happened to her? How can you do it?'

I pull myself back in. I think of my mantra. I can feel my blood boiling, but it won't help. There isn't any money, so this is all Stella will be entitled to, unless in the near future we miraculously come out of austerity – or stop using limited existing funding to pay for private fostering services.

Finally, Dave pipes up to diffuse the moment. 'We all know that the effects of childhood sexual abuse tend to develop and implode when a young person hits puberty. What Louise – and I think all of us here – would like to know, is what plans you have for her future.'

Tony says, 'At this stage, Dave, and with the economics as they are, we really cannot say with any degree of certainty. We can only do what we can.'

Trudy and Tony exchange a look.

And then they drop their bombshell.

'And that's why we have decided to put Stella up for adoption.' Trudy delivers it. As though it is nothing at all. An aside. I want to scream again. My body feels like it's going to explode. I wish there was a garden and some bins to tip over.

'But why?' I hear myself saying. 'Why? Why? This is not what Stella needs right now. Have you *met* Stella? Have you actually met her? Spent time with her? Got to know her? She is happy with us, really happy with us, and actually beginning to settle. She feels safe with us. It's through being in our care that we have begun to get to the heart of her troubles. And I know how to help her. I have worked with "CSE" children before. I understand what's required and how the abuse can manifest. I want the chance to continue working with Stella. I've been fighting for her. She trusts me. She trusts us. She is at home with us.' It is the longest speech that has been made since we walked into this oppressive room. I look from one to another of the other professionals gathered here, but Julie and Nick don't have any sway over these kinds of decisions. I repeat my entreaty and direct it towards Trudy, 'I just want the chance—'

She cuts me off. 'I'm sure you do, Louise, but we strongly feel that a secure placement in an adoptive home will be best for Stella at this time.'

I want to shout out of the window at the top of my voice, from the rooftop, to anyone who will listen to me, '*That's because adoption does not cost you a penny*!'

But I don't. This whole meeting has been hostile from the start. It feels that this decision is a personal attack, as well as a result of the budget cuts. I need to be rational and present my arguments logically. I feel that I'm part of a nest of Russian dolls. I take off the outer, impassioned, desperate one, and become a different version, one who offers another perspective. My voice drops down a notch. I am serious, and reasonable.

So I don't mention the cost. Instead I say, 'But if she is adopted, and her recent behaviours begin to emerge again, how do you know that the adopters can deal with it? You know as well as I do that adoptive parents often lack the training and expertise required in a case such as this.' I hate describing Stella as a 'case', but I am trying to appeal to them using their own language. 'You know, too, that adoptive parents are pretty much left alone to get on with it by local authorities.' I try to stop myself from thinking about what happens when adoption breaks down, which it does frequently during the teenage years, because of the delayed effects of things like foetal damage and sexual abuse: if the child goes back into fostering, adoptive parents are isolated and abandoned by the local authority. Adoptive parents can often end up feeling punished by the authorities for earlier trauma that isn't their fault and in which they played no part. I don't have to say all this because nobody interrupts to challenge that point.

I carry on, unstoppable now. 'Is that what we are saying we want for little Stella? What if they can't cope and the adoption breaks down? She will end up back in the fostering system in a much worse state than she is now.'

Tony, whose insouciant, inappropriate quiff is really beginning to annoy me now, says, 'Louise, you are a pessimist.'

So, we're getting personal now, are we? 'No, Tony. Generally my glass is half-full. But I am a realist and I know all too well that when budget constraints dictate a child's care plan, it is never 'for the best', as you have tried to suggest.'

There is another pause, which again I feel compelled to fill. 'Why can't she just stay with us?'

Uh oh. I have climbed in to the next Russian doll, the plaintive one.

Trudy says, 'OK, Louise. Cards on the table, then. Would you be prepared to adopt Stella?'

I can't make a life-changing decision like that without talking to Lloyd and to the rest of the family. How dare she? That wasn't even 'on the table' as a possibility until a few moments ago.

Stella's big eyes appear in my own mind's eye. I say, 'Maybe.' And then, 'You honestly can't expect me to give you an answer now.'

Julie jumps in. 'Can we go back to the case at hand, and the original purpose of this meeting, please?' Then adds, pointedly, 'We are already running very late.'

To me she gives a warm smile. I think that was a rescue manoeuvre, and once again I find myself feeling very grateful towards the WPC.

Nick says, 'Our first priority is to ensure that Stella is safe and, given the context in this instance, we believe that while living with Louise and her family, she is.' He is good. He is somehow managing to make it sound as though he has influence or even jurisdiction over the decision. 'The other important factor is that there should not be any further contact with her mother – though while Shannon remains missing that would obviously be unlikely.'

Dave follows up with, 'So, shall we agree then, that while the investigations are happening it would be in Stella's best interest to stay put with the Allens? Perhaps at a later date we can than revisit the adoption.'

I want to hug both of them. It feels good to have people batting for my team for once. For one glorious moment I think that it is all going to happen as Dave suggests.

Until Trudy says, 'No, I'm afraid that's not possible. Jo Sykes will be in soon from the adoption team to update us on Stella's adoption.'

It is like a physical blow.

I narrow my eyes. Now mean Russian doll comes out. 'Your use of the term 'update' would suggest that you're now giving us more information about something we already know. The reality is, Trudy, this is the first we have heard about it.'

She says, 'Well, you know now.'

I want to punch her. That is my first instinct. Thankfully, physically violent Russian doll remains locked up inside. But this Trudy really seems as though she is a nasty young woman who wants to deliberately challenge and upset me. She is also clearly flirting with Tony – the coquettish flicks of her hair and 'private' smiles haven't gone unnoticed by me, or by Tony – who, if he wasn't having a midlife crisis, might perhaps be chairing this meeting more fairly and effectively.

There is a knock at the door. An older, mousey woman puts her head around the door. She says 'Hello?' rather uncertainly, before finding the courage to step into the room. 'I am Jo Sykes from adoption. We have put a national call out for Stella, and have received a fair bit of interest so far, that Trudy and myself will pursue.' She nods enthusiastically at each of us, as though this is good news.

I can't believe what I'm hearing. This was all a done deal before we even walked into the room. I ask, 'Where?'

Trudy says, 'Near Manchester. A family have made a serious expression of interest, and that's good because as we all know, older children are hard to adopt for one reason or another.'

Tony thanks Jo Sykes, who scurries away back to her shared glass office with another nod as she closes the door behind her. I am reeling. The news – and how far progressed the adoption process seems to be already – leaves me utterly dumbfounded.

Remotely, and muffled as though I am underwater and only part-hearing, Tony says, 'Okay, I think we are all done here.' He snaps his folder of notes shut with a finality that I am not ready for, and then it is all business and practicality. 'Nick, you will keep us in the loop about how the investigations are developing. Julie, you can do a handover to the lead of the Future Journeys programme and report to Trudy, please. Oh, and thank you, Louise for all that you are doing for Stella.' This last is almost an afterthought. And Tony and Trudy are out of that door so fast that I hardly have time to open my mouth.

Dave looks at me. 'You did all that you could, Louise.'

I ask him outright, 'Did you know about this?' I can't believe it, but I have to know.

'No, Louise, I didn't. I truly didn't – and I'm very sorry.'

There is nothing more to say.

We part ways at the reception exit.

I'm in a daze and turn the wrong way out of the building. I notice Nick and Julie waiting along the path. I'm clearly in shock and I can't remember where I parked my car.

They walk back towards me. I really feel as though I don't know where I am. Nick is chewing some gum very fast. He looks at me, searchingly, and says, 'We didn't see that one coming.'

I just about manage to shake my head. That's the correct response in this sort of situation, I believe. Though right now, I don't even think I know which way is up.

'Are you okay, Louise?'

I look right at him but I only see a blur, because tears have filled my eyes. 'No, I'm not. I'm not at all. I'm not quite sure what just happened. Or why it just happened?'

Julie puts her hand on my arm. 'Louise, I don't know why I was asked to do the handover. Frankly, I have other things to do and it's really your role. When I get the email from the Lead of Future Journeys I will make sure she has your details.'

Nick says again, 'Are you okay?'

I know that I will have to be, somehow.

'Yes, yes, I'm fine.' I say, with more conviction than I feel. 'I just need to process what just happened.'

We say goodbye. I walk around the streets for a long time looking for my car.

Chapter 14

I am utterly in pieces when I finally get home. Afterwards, I have no memory of a journey that I must have driven on auto-pilot. Lloyd is pragmatic and, after multiple cups of tea and a pile of tissues, he manages to talk me round into thinking that it might be the right thing for Stella. He is placating in the way that he agrees the whole thing has been handled very badly and very insensitively. But it is not the first time we have been excluded from the plans of the child in our care. The professionals can sometimes overlook the fact that the foster carers know the child better than any of them. Lloyd and I became so beaten down with things like this in the past that we joined the foster care workers' union, an organisation now known as the Independent Foster Carers Alliance.

Within a few days I have managed to re-orientate my thinking towards generating a plan for Stella to leave us. I tell myself that the adoptive family may well have the where-withal to locate adequate funding for the therapies that Stella will need, and set about researching what might be available and how it might be accessed. The money can be found, sometimes, if you know where to look.

I begin an extensive literature review, looking at the types of therapy that have been most effective in helping children who have been sexually abused. My university connections mean that I am able to gain access to the latest research, in the era before open access. I am most interested – and sometimes the crossest – about some practices within the 'talking therapies'. This is an umbrella term that incorporates things like group therapies, counselling and cognitive behavioural therapy (CBT). I become familiar with the big names researching in this field. The literature is often dense, and sometimes impenetrable, but I persevere. I don't always understand everything that I read, but I drive Lloyd mad quoting stuff at him.

The impact of sexual abuse on children is, of course, difficult to measure, and I start trying to read up systematically on what work has been done in this area, too. I find myself conducting internet searches for things like 'resilience factors' and 'transactional analysis' and am particularly interested in what children themselves have to say about the therapy they receive. I discover, personally, that I am shifting away from talking therapies and the way that they are seen as a cure-all, mainly because children who have been abused are hyper-vigilant and good at reading the signals around them, and will say anything to please the adult.

Given my art background, I also find myself drawn to papers on creative therapies like play therapy, drama therapy and, of course, the thing that got me through, though not just in a formal group: art therapy.

I look at the contrast between what is available privately compared with what might come via the authorities. Perhaps Stella's adoptive family won't need to be tenacious about securing funding and will simply be wealthy enough to pay for what she needs. I work on best-case scenarios for her future. I can't allow myself to think in any other way.

I tell myself that the adoptive family is busy doing the same as me. Why not? But in case they aren't, I begin to put a file together for them. Julie has said that she will press for me to do the handover. This will become the most informed handover in the history of social care, I tell myself. It is the very least I can do.

But the more I read, the more I realise how important the carer is. I begin to understand that you don't have to be an 'expert' to help a child. Just because you are not a trained therapist doesn't mean that you can't be a listener, and it also doesn't mean that you can't maximise the resources around you. Just by doing all this reading I already feel in a better position to help Stella than I did when I was acting instinctively and in the moment, and most people can manage a bit of reading.

I am an artist, and Stella therefore has access to a range of art materials and, through me, techniques. I think back to the various art projects she has completed, and understand how beneficial this was for her. I feel more confident about my own abilities, and know that you really don't have to be a specialist to do this job. Time and patience are key.

Meanwhile, WPC Julie Watters is as good as her word, and keeps us in the loop with regular updates. Shannon remains in hiding and this makes it easy for court proceedings to continue uninterrupted. Stella's father is in jail and her mother is missing. They even make an attempt to track down Shannon's adoptive parents, but it transpires that Shannon has been using her birth name, not theirs, and so they are not found either. The judge puts Stella on a full care order, otherwise known in foster parlance as a 'Section 47.' Section 47 refers to the relevant bit of the 1989 Children Act, which relates to enquiries undertaken by the local authority when a concern arises that a child may be suffering, or is likely to suffer, significant harm – but has somehow come to mean the removal of a child.

For Stella, in practical terms, this means she will remain in the care system until she is 18 years old, unless she is adopted, in which case she will live as a birth child in a family. There is no chance that she will ever be returned to her parents.

The family near Manchester that Trudy seemed very certain about come to visit. Afternoon tea is arranged at my house, so that the couple, who are called Lawrence and Lydia, can meet Stella. We avoid saying to Stella exactly why they are coming – other than to say hello. We definitely avoid the preferred phrase of the children's social services, who already call them Stella's 'forever family'. At this stage I feel that would simply be cruel, as we all know nothing is written in stone – and what is 'forever' anyway? My own unfortunate pedigree in abuse, neglect and rejection makes me suspicious of a word like 'forever' and even more so of the saccharine 'forever family' as a moniker.

The moment I open the door to them, I feel that they are the wrong people, but I know that this is my innate bias and desire not to give her up, so for Stella, and for her future, I am friendly and helpful. The visit is awkward right from the start, however much I try and smooth it – largely because the situation itself is awkward.

And this is intensified when Lawrence says, 'Her eyes are rather large, aren't they? Does she have any processing problems?' when Stella and Lily have run off to get a toy from Stella's room.

I'm not going to dignify his question with an answer, so pretend that I haven't heard as I busy myself with taking the scones from the oven.

'What big eyes, you have, my dear,' Lydia jokes, in imitation of a character from *Little Red Riding Hood*, and I suddenly begin thinking of her as a wolf. But a wolf in sheep's clothing. She just has nothing much about her. Where is the spirit that Stella will need, for someone to fight on her behalf?

'Shall we go to the park, Stella?' the wolf asks, when the girls return.

I had been told by Trudy that they would want to do this, but I find it hard just letting her go off with two strangers. It just seems wrong. Stella, wide-eyed and polite, just nods and goes along with it. She looks a little scared when she realises that Lily isn't coming with her, but dutifully does as she is told. I deflect the beseeching look that she gives me as they leave the house together and offer a reassuring one in return.

Afterwards, I am amazed that Trudy does not ask me for any feedback from Stella herself; they are only interested in what the potential adopters said and thought. It doesn't seem the right way round.

We are all anxious and, as always, Lloyd somehow manages to keep a steady tiller on our family's ship while we are left not knowing anything for nearly two weeks. Every few days we email Trudy and cc Tony and Dave – nothing. Eventually we hear that the Manchester couple have changed their minds and will not be adopting Stella after all. It is done in the form of a short, formal single-line email simply informing us that the adopters have pulled out. I email back and ask why.

There is no response.

I don't mind, though. My relief is great. Whatever my prejudices, Lydia and Lawrence were not right for her. But, after Trudy and Tony's cavalier approach to the adoption of Stella, they actually find it difficult to find other adopters. Older children, rather than young babies, are much harder to find adoptive families for. With Stella's needs and history she is quite a big ask for many families, who want a child who is simpler.

This makes me sad. All children need a long-term place-ment, and whether adopted or fostered, they have trauma – and therefore work to do. Dave is getting closer and closer to leaving. He doesn't say that he is letting go, but we sense it as he thins down his help and avoids making promises or taking on any new responsibilities. We feel rather adrift, surrounded by uncertainty. All goes very quiet on the adoption front. When we ask Dave, his candidness has gone and the standard responses return.

His view is, apparently, 'Oh, it's much harder to place an older child.' I hope that the authorities have come to their senses and like to think that they have had second thoughts because of Stella's complex history, and perhaps a fear of what might lie ahead. I also feel resentful that I have been made to feel that we have fallen short, somehow, that we are not good enough. This makes me angry.

Because, when all is said and done, Stella is now a part of our family. We want her here. We want to be the ones to care for her. We want her.

The longer the uncertainty, the more thrills and spills there are for the emotional rollercoaster ride that we seem to have found ourselves on. But we somehow manage to do what all good foster carers do: we smile and keep going and pretend that all is well. We are the swans who look fine – but underneath our legs are paddling very quickly just to make sure that we stay afloat.

The protective layer that I try to wrap around my heart is clearly faulty. Stella continues to work her way in there. And so, after another few weeks of becoming increasingly attached to Stella – and her to us – we get a new email from Trudy. There is another adopter wanting to meet Stella. Now it feels even worse. Now I am even more defensive than I was a month ago. How is it only a month? And now I feel even more protective than I ever did before. I email straight back with many questions. All are ignored. Again I have to arrange tea at home in order for Stella to meet the adopter. Adopter, singular. Just the one? This already bothers me. Where is the family that she needs?

Trudy seems to systematically ignore anything I have written: it is a gift, it truly is, how she is able to do this. Instead, she simply emails me with the agreed day and time of the visit. I feel put upon in the same way that I did when contact visits were arranged with Shannon. As though I am not allowed to have any kind of commitments or life beyond the foster child, that Saturday at 3pm is happening, regardless of what other family commitments we might have. And then I try to rationalise my own negative feelings towards whoever it is who will be turning up at my house at the weekend. It isn't their fault. They are doing a good thing.

We go through the process, almost mechanically, again. I manage the knowledge that Stella has. This is just someone else to meet, and Stella is used to it. She will be personable and polite, I have no doubt. On the Friday, just the day before the Saturday when we have the appointment, I am given a name: Danny. I am curious. Danny? With a 'y', not an 'i.' This is a man, then? On his own? I don't like this at all.

Saturday comes, as these days have a way of doing, even though I don't want them to. Between us all we manage to keep the house as calm as possible. We make it feel like a friend is dropping by, even though Danny is a stranger to us all. We slightly ignore the formal tea thing and just keep it relaxed. I don't want to bake another tray of scones for another wolf, anyway.

The doorbell goes. I look at Lloyd, who does his 'Here we go again' face. With some trepidation I head to the door. I have tried to avoid picturing 'Danny', but even so, I am surprised. There is a large bulk waiting behind the glass. I open the door to see a smiley, slightly greying man. There is a ruddy colour to his cheeks that give him a healthy, wholesome look. Though he is of medium height, his build is indeed generous. He has a touch of Father Christmas about him, albeit no beard. The warmth he projects is both reassuring and contagious. He is wearing a smart green corduroy jacket over dark, expensive jeans. He is holding a beautiful box of cakes tied with a red ribbon. He reaches out and shakes my hand.

In he comes, and I find that somehow, against all my intentions, he becomes lovely. Because he *is* lovely. Dotty is happy around him from the get go. When I ask him to sit down while I put the kettle on, she jumps into his lap and turns herself into a needy dog-baby. He is unperturbed, and happily sits and nurses her while we chat. Lloyd comes in, raises his eyebrows at Dotty's position and shakes his hand.

When he sits down, conversation between them opens up easily. There seems no need for the 'how was the journey and which roads and motorways did you choose?' chat. I feel myself die slightly inside whenever these conversations start, but today I don't. I notice that our kitchen is full of chatter, and soon full of children wanting to see who is here and what's going on.

Lily has no idea why Danny is here, but she starts chatting and wants to show him her guinea pigs – which she does with the aid of Stella. They are a good 20 minutes and I get the feeling that there may also be some guinea-pig-nursing going on, courtesy of Danny.

When they come back in the tea has brewed. Danny does a quick headcount around the room and says, 'Phew!' wiping his brow rid of the mock-perspiration. He says, 'I am pleased that I got the number right: four children and three adults; let's tuck in.' The cake box with the ribbons is opened to reveal what looks like a hand-crafted and individual fresh cream selection. Stella has her eye on a cream horn that Lily has also spotted – but with grace, Stella lets her have it and chooses an apricot slice instead. The boys are true to form and are in and out with their cakes with the stealth of Ninja warriors.

My voice follows them out of the door. 'Don't you take those cakes upstairs; I don't want crumbs everywhere!'

'No, mum,' they call, feet already clattering their way up the staircase.

Situation normal. Even though it isn't. Or shouldn't be, at least.

It isn't long before the girls head off to play outside. Again, this feels right. They aren't standing on formality because a visitor is here; neither is there any suggestion of Danny spending time alone with Stella. He makes no noises about wanting to take Stella to the park or for a walk. In the end I ask him if he would like to, in case it's just that he is too polite to raise it.

He looks at me kindly, 'No, I think not. I think that would be too much for any child. I have met her, and for now that's more than enough.'

So there is no need for me to let her go off to the park with a stranger this time – although, in fairness, Danny already feels like an old friend.

The departure of the girls means that I can talk to Dan (somehow he has gone from Danny to Dan without anyone really saying anything). Lloyd is still in the kitchen, resisting DIY duties. Maintenance is a perpetual problem given that we live in an old house, built in 1640, with many extensions and added-on bits since. There is always something that needs to be done and, as Lloyd is keen to point out, I am very good at compiling lists of exactly what those things might be, thereby always ensuring that there are plenty of chores. Lloyd spends much of his time building or painting, and lately has turned his hand to woodwork too. It saves us a fortune but rather ties us to the house. This is not usually a problem, as the children love being at home. When I was a child I was always looking for any excuse to get out, but I can't seem to get ours out. I'm happy when they seem content.

Dan is happy to tell us all about himself and his background. He is single and father to three older, adopted children. He set up an engineering business when he was in his twenties and it became very big and successful. He always wanted children of his own, he tells us, but could never meet the right person. He has been a dad for 11 years now and loves it.

'I do cheat, though.'

His definition of cheating is to have a housekeeper, who is also a great friend of the family.

From his wallet, Dan pulls out multiple pictures of his other children. They are all of different heritages. I look at him with renewed interest. This excites me. Personally, I have always been interested in looking after children from other countries. I would have loved the research into their heritage and immersion in other cultures.

Danny explains how he uses an adoption charity and does not go through local authorities. He has worked with the same charity for each child placed in his family. He shows us pictures of his home, the bedroom that could be Stella's. The house is large and tastefully decorated. This man clearly has a lot of wealth, but he is not using it to make more – he is using it for a greater good.

I make us all a fresh pot of tea as conversation moves to Stella's psych report. It is Dan who brings this up first. I feel my stomach twinge as I feel the future shame on Stella's behalf. Dan's language is honest and forthright but not in any way patronising. He doesn't call Stella a 'poor child', or say, 'this is very serious' or mutter that it will be difficult to deal with. Instead, he explains that he and the charity have a plan in place. He explains that he has looked into funding through the charity and has made a commitment that if the different approaches seem to be helpful for Stella then he will fund them for as long as she needs them. I know it is a cliche to talk about emotions being a rollercoaster, but I now want to cry with happiness on her behalf. This is exactly what Stella needs.

I ask him if he feels worried. He shakes his head almost imperceptibly and smiles.

'My oldest child, Maya, was found next to a bin in a village in China. She was four years old and had been abused in every way imaginable. So yes, I am worried. I don't walk in to this with my eyes closed. The reality is that it does not bother me as much as it does them. I haven't been the one to suffer. It has not happened to me. My children are amazing and I have made myself available for each of them.'

Wealthy and wise. Is it possible that Dan is too good to be true?

'I've done a great deal of research over the years. When my business was up and running and no longer felt like a challenge, I changed direction and did an MA in this field – because I wanted, needed to know more. But after that, I chose not to pursue academia. Maya is not an object of scientific enquiry, she is my child. I hope that Stella can be, too. None of them are my subjects: they are my children.'

I sit back, stunned by what he has said. I am in awe of this man, what he has achieved and the way that he has gone about it. I know that I want to be his friend, and I think that he has the resources and the knowledge to be able to make Stella happy.

There is a break in the conversation. He gives me a little sideways look and hesitates before he says, 'You're Louise Allen, author of *Thrown Away Child*, aren't you?' He looks a little bashful, as he asks.

'Yes.' On top of everything else he has done his homework about me, too.

'I don't have the first-hand experience that you do. But I have other things to offer. You will understand why I love my life, and what I do. What I am able to do for children like Stella.'

I nod. 'I am happy to hear that you do. Vulnerable children need to live in a relaxed home. It's pretty effective as therapy in itself.'

If it is an act, then he has totally won me over with it. Part of me feels as though I want to stand up and applaud. But I don't believe for one moment that it is an act. He is intelligent, articulate and everything he says seems well considered.

Eventually it's time for Dan to leave. We go outside to look for the children. Lily and Stella come crashing into us, laughing and giggling. Stella is such a beautiful child – and now has the chance of a life and an inheritance. Standing here is the guardian of her heart and of her future.

I let go of all my concerns.

'Your friend Danny-Dan was nice, Louise,' Stella tells me when he has gone. It is unlike her to volunteer an opinion without being asked directly, and I take it as another auspicious sign.

Danny-Dan comes to visit many more times. I encourage him to do some art with Stella, at times setting them up together in my studio and leaving them to it. His creative efforts aren't up to much, but he can see how important it is for Stella to have an outlet like this. Though she never quite repeats the stark sketches from that day at my kitchen table, Dan recognises its powerful therapeutic quality and potential. I offer other ideas and advice, all of which he seems grateful to hear. He promises to fund more art therapy, and to investigate drama therapy.

He tells me that he is keen to invest in TA, Transactional Analysis, a model of support that works around personality. I am a fan of it myself because it is built around the philosophy that everyone is fundamentally OK, has their own capacity to think for themselves, and considers their own power to change their future and destiny, whatever has happened to them. To me it is so much more refreshing than beginning from a starting point of damage and the idea of something to fix. I find the personal responsibility element of TA empowering. Dan is also considering EMDR for Stella – Eye Movement Desensitisation Reprocessing. I am less familiar with the fine detail of this kind of treatment myself, but I know many carers who have funded this personally and the benefits are good. It's a method for encouraging the brain to process traumatic and distressing memories and experiences to reduce their influence and impact in the here and now. Dan has really done his homework. Not only does he have the knowledge, but he also has the financial clout to make this happen where it is not available as a funded option.

On the third or fourth visit Dan brings with him his other children for us to meet. It is a wonderful occasion, a beautiful day. The house is full of energy and laughter from the moment they get to us. His children are amazing in themselves, but particularly in their outward-looking mindset and determination to welcome Stella into their number. We can also see that they love Dan dearly, and he loves them. They arrive in a shiny Range Rover, spilling out from in it in a tumble of colour and life. He must have a whole fleet of vehicles. Previously when he had been on his own he was in a Porsche. (I know, because Lloyd looked out of the window, mouth open.)

It is the Porsche that he brings back when he comes to take Stella away to her new home. Of course, I am sad about parting, but I know it really is for the best. And I also know that it is not the end. Dan really has become a friend, and friends visit each other, so we will be seeing plenty more of Stella. I am so pleased about this. Often children in care might experience multiple 'homes' that they stay in briefly but that might never be returned to. That will not happen in this case. Much healthier for Stella to maintain the relationships that she has built up, with Lily for instance.

In the top of her suitcase sits the little framed picture that we made from the dried flowers when she first arrived – a little memory of her welcome into our family as she departs for a new one. She climbed onto a stool in her bedroom when we were packing and took it down from the wall herself. I am pleased that she wants to take it with her. I hope that we have made as much of an impression on her as she has on us, and am again reminded of the two-way nature of this fostering cycle.

I wave Stella off in the open-top sports car on a glorious evening. Danny-Dan revs the engine as though they are in pole position at the start of a Formula One race. We are having something of an Indian Summer this year. I think what a lucky girl she is to have found Dan.

Then I think about what joy she has brought to our household over the last few months and I add to that thought: what a lucky man Dan is to have found Stella.

Epilogue

There is the thud on the doormat that Stella has been waiting for. She shifts herself out towards the hallway. She got up early this morning so that she could be ready for the time when the postman delivered. Her movements towards the hall are bulky and awkward. Gone is the bird-like frame that once so defined her. Battles with food and periods of over-eating have dominated her teenage years.

Tancred, a little white terrier, bounces along beside her. He is such a loyal little dog, and although he is a very different breed from Shark Attack all those years ago, she feels an affinity with the animal. She is well aware that Tancred can't possibly understand her, but on another level, he seems to know exactly what is going on and be able to sense and respond to her mood. He was a rescue, just like her, and is missing an eye from who knows what horrors before Danny allowed Stella to bring him home. She will get Tancred his breakfast in a moment, when she has read what this morning's post has to bring. She is able to keep Tancred fit and healthy and full of beans, if not always herself.

Stella has had a range of therapies and treatments over the years, some of which have been more successful than others. She enjoys the art and drama sessions the most. But when you find out that you have been part of a national paedophile ring, the most expensive therapies on the market can't take away the reality of the events themselves. Stella doesn't like the word 'victim', though she has come to understand and accept the fact that that is what she was.

None of it was her fault – she knows that now.

In prison the first time, Terry became involved in child pornography, and when he came out he had known exactly where to find a suitable child: in his own home. His own daughter made the perfect subject, as he had ready access to her. Later, Shannon also got involved because it was more lucrative than being on the game. Better to prostitute your child than yourself, Stella thinks, bitterly. But Stella also knows that this is an unhelpful cycle of thinking, and so she shuts it off. Nothing can undo what has already happened, but Stella knows that she is able to take charge of what happens next in her life. It is why she has put herself forward for the apprenticeship, even though she doesn't really think that she is good enough.

From the end of the hallway she recognises the one envelope she is waiting for immediately. She doesn't really think that the news will be good. She is not naturally confident, and struggles with self-esteem and anxiety. Why should they want her when there are plenty of other 18-year-olds out there who might do the job much better? Thankfully, the panic attacks that she suffered from all the way through puberty have now more or less subsided, but she knows that she can still be taken over by that overwhelming sensation and then she feels the tightness in her chest, her lungs closing up, her power to breathe all gone.

But she has done the hard part, she reminds herself. The achievement of the qualification in the first place surprised her. Who knew that she would be able to gain an NVQ? Little Stella Artois-Bennett? Well, not so little these days. But it is two weeks since the envelope bearing *that* good news dropped onto the mat, and the possibilities that it offers are finally beginning to sink in.

It wasn't her first choice. She initially wanted to train as a nursery teacher, but her dad cleverly steered her away from that, tactfully resisting Stella's social workers' and teachers' suggestions that she consider going into early years childcare. Her dad was concerned that a young woman who had been so traumatised as a child should not work with children. He felt from learning and observing her trauma that if she felt unsafe she might enter one of her quiet, internal meltdown phases where she couldn't speak or explain how she felt. He was concerned that if she was hit or hurt by a child – that might only be by accident – her behaviour could be unpredictable, and might have consequences that could affect her adult working life. He is probably right. And now she is waiting to hear about whether or not she has been successful. Actually, if it hadn't been for Danny-Dan, her adopted father, going all out to find her this position, she knows that she probably wouldn't have had the drive to chase it herself. She bends down and reaches for the thick white envelope.

It's open in her shaking hands before she quite knows what she is doing. The words are a little bit blurry, but yes, she will be going to work in the local veterinary practice, where she can begin the apprenticeship for veterinary nursing. Her feelings soar upwards. The anxiety and depression that have clouded days and weeks at a time, regularly paralysing her, lift.

It is only up the road, so she can still live at home. This is Danny's plan, so that he can carry on being there for her. He knows only too well how to help her through the dark times. She hugs the letter to her chest. She has a qualification *and* a job. More than a job: a career. Working with animals. And you can care for animals and they don't say or do things that are hurtful. Stella remembers the warmth of Shark Attack, and the comfort of Dotty and Douglas.

And she has a family. She takes a deep breath. Danny has been instrumental in making this happen. She wants so much to make him proud of her.

'Dad? Dad! Guess what?' Stella calls up the stairs where her father is getting ready for the day.

She meets him halfway up the stairs and throws herself into his arms.

'I got it! I got it!'

He kisses the top of her head.

'You did? Yes, you did! Of course you did. Well done, Stella. You deserve it. Show me.'

She watches as he reads the letter.

'Shall we tell the others?'

Maya is on her gap year, travelling in Australia. Paula is at university. Freddie, who like Stella is a lover of animals, is already at work, having risen early for a shift on a local farm.

Telling the others means adding a picture in the family WhatsApp group. Danny puts his arm around Stella's shoulders to take the selfie. In the background behind them, on the wall just above Stella, is a little framed selection of pressed sweet peas and violets.

'Hold the letter up so that they can see what it says!'

She will never really like having her photograph taken, but she is learning that to be valued for yourself, on your own terms, and especially in these moments of quiet achievement, is very, very different from being 'valued' for a physical attribute, or for what is being done *to* you. She puts the letter right up underneath her chin so that her body is hidden from the camera. It is not a body she is proud of. It is not a body that will ever bear children: there was too much damage done to her sexual organs for that. And recovery is a long way off. More operations lie ahead.

Click.

Danny passes the phone to her for approval.

'Not bad,' she admits. It's ok when it's just her face. Her eyes, she knows, are her most startling feature.

She looks over his shoulder as he types the message. The plaudits come pinging back from her siblings almost instantly. It is great to have a family, a tribe who understand her. And inside she glows from the caption that accompanied the picture:

So proud of Stella today. It's really happening for her now!

Afterword

I have finished writing Stella's story and I am still here with my laptop thinking about what to say to you. I notice the hot and cold nips in the air, the long shadows of our house on the lawn arriving earlier each day. Autumn is definitely here along with the countdown festivities to the build-up of Christmas. As foster carers, we hold our breath at Mothers' Day, Fathers' Day, Easter, birthdays and Christmas. They serve as annual reminders to our children of their old lives and the muddle we all find ourselves in. In our house Mothers' day is kept low-key: my children make me a card, but we don't make a fuss because our foster children find it hard not being with *their* mothers, no matter what went on. It is a narrative that is hard to escape because according to the adverts, we only ever have one mother and she is nothing short of an angel – but we know that's not true, don't we?

Christmas is even worse. It can be the most harrowing of times for foster children because it can be too much for them. Yet I know of foster carers who put their foster children into respite whilst they celebrate Christmas with just their own children and grandchildren. Perhaps it is a form of self-preservation. Perhaps they do not want repeat of a previous stressful Christmas. I try not to judge, but sometimes I can't help myself. If we are lucky and have a social worker sensible enough to arrange contact with the child's birth family just as school finishes – allowing the child time to settle before Christmas with minimum external interference – the child can just about relax and join in. But it's a big ask of them.

It would be nice to think that careful planning was a regular strategy for a happy placement, but, sadly, it's not always like that. Social workers also need to get ready for the holiday. We have had contact visits and phone calls take place on Christmas Eve and even on Christmas Day,– a scenario that only results in angry, sad, resentful upset children over Christmas. The same thing happens with ill-advised contact in the middle of the summer holidays or worse, just before they return to school, causing more upset.

If you are a social worker reading this, then I beg you to plan carefully. We need our foster children to feel safe and calm at these annual events and holidays. We must do all we can to prevent the placement breaking down.

For my little blended family we move towards Halloween – the official scariest time of the year. In my experience, this festivity has the least impact on our foster children. I wonder if that's because our foster children have seen and experienced much scarier things, more than most of us could ever imagine. I think of a little boy whose drunken mother thought it would be funny to wake him up dressed as Freddy Krueger after letting him watch horror films at six years old. He still has nightmares. But for us autumn is not just Halloween and fireworks displays, it's spiders.

Every child who has come into our home, no matter how old, has been scared of spiders. Not like how most children are scared of our little housemates – but really scared. The little tiny ones, the friendly ones, the daddy long legs (or, as a child from Yorkshire called them, 'Jimmy Spinners'), the ones who mind their own business in the corner of a room, or the big hairy ones that come up through the bathroom plug hole.

I have been woken by the cries, or screams, of children reacting to a spider in the darkness. Perhaps it is their past life trauma interrupting their dreams. With stinging eyes I try to soothe and console them; to distract them from their spiders, which I think represent other, darker fears. But if they see a real spider, I have to go through the ritual removal process of using the blue extended brush I keep on the landing for this precise purpose. I carefully coax the little critters out and place conkers along the windows and mix essential oils such as citrus, cedarwood, tea tree and lavender and squirt them round the room. After many years of fostering – and flushing out the spiders – my previous Buddhist gentleness disappeared. I began to squash them and get them out as fast as I could, in order to get back to my own sleep. A good night's sleep is one of a foster carer's most important assets. But there is a sting as

I hear a child's voice whisper, 'Mrs Spider, I have killed your children.' It's what a happy, well-adjusted child said in my car as we were on our way with a number of Vincent's friends to a birthday Chinese buffet treat. It has made me think twice when I encounter an arachnid.

When Jackson started nursery school he, too, suddenly became scared of spiders: screaming when he saw them, crying for me to remove them. He did not have this fear before he went to nursery – it was something he picked up pretty quickly when he began. I was cross when I learnt it was the young nursery nurses transferring their fears onto the children. I registered my dismay, in what I hope was a supportive way, to the manager – who told me she was also scared of spiders. I was frustrated. I didn't want my child to be scared of little bugs that live with us every day; and whose cobwebs are so fascinating, especially in late autumn in the hedges after the morning damp clings to their shapes and amplifies their size. We looked at these spider villages on the way to the nursery. I would point them out to Jackson, who looked in wonder at this marvellous sight. I didn't want my children carrying and mimicking other people's fears and missing out on all this magic.

I fought back against my son's new fear. I made paper spiders with him. I named the spiders in our house and made sure that we said 'hello' and 'good night' to them. My son soon lost his fear of spiders when he moved on to the reception class at our local primary school, where they embraced creepy crawlies. I told him, as I do all my children, the story of my tiny kitchen in my old flat. Before I was married I lived on the top floor of an old Victorian building where I loved to cook dinners for my friends. I had one very dear friend called Helen. She was a singer. She was hilarious and theatrical. I adored her, but she was a busybody in my kitchen, unable to cook herself but always giving me advice. She picked and nibbled at the ingredients whilst I prepared meals. One day she screamed after noticing a big spider in its web above the kitchen door. She never came past the threshold again. But when Gilbert (as we named him) left, I replaced him with a fake black plastic spider from the toyshop, to keep it that way. Helen, along with my other girlfriends, would stand with wine glass in hand, chatting and laughing in the doorway, I had room to move and the food was safe. Sorry Helen! I feel guilty that I took advantage of your fear. But do we take advantage of other people's fears. I am now becoming more aware of what the fear of spiders means to foster children.

One night, I was sitting with Stella soothing her (because, of course, she too had the spider fear), gently patting her back through the duvet because we have been advised and trained not to touch the children directly (please let's not go there, I can get quite upset and cross when everything inside me is wanting to give a child a proper, big, squidgy hug), when it occurred to me that this over-reaction from our foster children about the spiders – and our response to it – is actually the summary of our jobs as foster carers: they want to feel rescued and we must help our foster children lose their fears. That's if they are with us long enough, of course.

But I'm also worried. Are rescuers the right people to be foster carers? Who are we to assume that we can be better parents? I realised pretty sharply after becoming a foster carer that to do any good at all, to apply my experience and knowledge and heart, I had to find a way to help bring about change to this broken system – which is why I write my books and campaign relentlessly for foster carers and foster children.

Being a parent is tough, hard work. At a time when the market has never been so full of parenting guidebooks, perhaps somewhat ironically, never have so many children been in care. As the *parent person* (that is the phrase I use when talking to my foster children) I have to be brave and say 'no' sometimes. I tell them, 'I have to not be your friend. I have friends as do you. I have to do right by you because I am the parent person, I am the adult. I attend parents' evenings. I sit up late waiting for you to return home dressed in my PJs and shoes ready to jump in the car at any moment. I make sure you have food and try to help you with your homework, even if that's just by making you a hot chocolate (because I seriously do not understand your homework). I will always try to do right by you!'

And I will keep on getting rid of the spiders. One at a time.

Acknowledgements

Thank you to my family – Lloyd, Jackson and Vincent Allen, Taryn and Chloe, Millie and Mitchell Cawte, Poppy; Jane Graham-Maw (my special agent); Theresa Gooda (a clever woman); Jo Sollis (my great editor); James Nicholls (my enabler and inspiration); Ronnie (the other me).

If you are interested in fostering or adoption, contact your local authority. If you search for 'Fostering' or 'Adoption' on the internet you will see many private and independent agencies advertising their services and amounts that you can earn. I suggest you talk to your local authority in the first instance, who will be able to give you realistic advice and support.

Families for Children is an independent, voluntary adoption agency based in the South West. We find and support adoptive families across Devon, Cornwall, Somerset & Dorset for vulnerable children waiting for adoptive families across the UK. As a specialist adoption agency, we understand the trauma and neglect that many of the children waiting to be adopted have suffered and the effects this can have on the child and whole family, some of which can be unknown for many years.

The support we provide to these families is vital, as having well-trained, prepared and supported families ensures that the children we place can have a happy and secure home life.

At any one time Families for Children are supporting 100 families and have to raise £300,000 per year to continue to provide these vital services.

www.familiesforchildren.org.uk

www.ifcalliance.co.uk

Abby's Story

Next in the Thrown Away Children series

By Louise Allen

Preview:

Chapter 1

Noise echoes around the gymnasium. The artificial light is bright and unforgiving.

Dozens of secondary school children dressed in identical pale blue polo-shirts and navy shorts dart about in organised chaos. Old-fashioned climbing apparatus stands dormant against the walls. The air is filled with shrieks, the squeaky noise of rubber trainers, and the thwack of nylon strings on shuttlecocks.

Lisa is in the middle of it all, down on the hard wooden floor snatching desperately at a breath she can't seem to get hold of.

'What's up? Can't you take the pace? Is my killer drop shot too much for you?' Simone calls out to her from the other side of the net.

On any normal day Lisa would have a smart reply for Simone's banter, but today, right now, in this truly horrible moment, nothing whatsoever comes into her mind apart from trying to find that breath. The fact that she has no air in her lungs makes reply impossible anyway. She closes her eyes for a moment, focusing on the complicated act of breathing and on controlling the sharp, sharp pain that stabs suddenly through her side.

When she opens her eyes again Lisa has trouble focusing on the other three badminton courts. There are doubles games going on around her, in varying degrees of competitiveness, but she can't make them out properly. Something odd seems to have happened to her vision. Everyone and everything has a blurred edge, as though some distorting filter has been applied to reality.

She feels totally detached from everything, all of a sudden. It is almost as though Lisa is no longer physically in the room, not part of this PE lesson. Perhaps the only way through this nightmare now is to pretend that it isn't happening, she thinks. To carry on pretending, as she has done for the last six months, ever since the horrible truth dawned on her.

Darting movements accompany the noise of laughter and whistles that continue to echo around the gym. Wednesday, period three. Double PE. Badminton. The world, school, is carrying on in the ordinary way that it does. Ordinary things are happening all around her.

But things are also happening *to* her. And those things are anything but ordinary.

Lisa finally manages to draw a breath from somewhere. She feels as though she is being pulled underwater but has snatched air at the surface. Nothing looks real. The whole room – the gym – also seems to be underwater. She can make out limbs and their bodies moving around the court spaces, but they look like insects, or seaweed – indistinct and inhuman. As do the students lined up on benches at the side awaiting their turn to play. They are little dark blobs on the edges of her vision, not people at all.

Ms Plant – with the emphasis firmly on 'Ms' – is there in the corner; Lisa can just about identify the teacher through squinting eyes bracing against pain. But stern Ms Plant isn't even sympathetic to a bit of period pain, so she isn't going to be an ally. She can't see the whistle strung below Ms Plant's neck but knows it's there, as it is every PE lesson. She knows that she will get into serious trouble in a minute, if she doesn't get up. Ms Plant hasn't seen her yet. The teacher is busy looking at something in her hand. Maybe a stopwatch. Yes. Stopwatch.

Time.

It is nearly lunchtime. *Hold on to that thought,* she tells herself. Lunchtime. Perhaps the brutal, stabbing pain that Lisa feels in her stomach is just hunger. It could be. Some food might sort all this out. That will be it: food. But now there is a similar sharp pain to the one in her abdomen over her right eye. That can't be from hunger. It feels as though someone has put an ice pick through her forehead and is twisting it around. She should take some paracetamol or ibuprofen. It is part hangover, perhaps. And part just having to deal with Year 9 PE, in her state. Usually exercise makes the pain go away. Not today.

'Get up, faker.'

Lisa hears Simone's voice but can't quite see her opponent and friend across the net, and can't seem to lift herself from the ancient parquet flooring. *Jesus. What the bloody hell is happening to me?* She thinks. *Get a grip. Everyone's looking.*

'Sorry, Lis – I didn't realise you were actually hurt. Did you twist something?' The voice is nearer now. Simone's tone has changed entirely and her face is wearing a concerned frown as she finally reaches Lisa. But Simone's approach also means that other people will notice.

Lisa gives up the struggle to focus properly. There is no point. Nothing will stay still. The students on and near the benches seem to be floating in the air, not sitting or walking at all. Now some of them are running forward to be near her.

'Miss, miss! I think Lisa's fainted.'

But she has not fainted. She is still acutely conscious, and that consciousness carries the weight of a terrible fear. The pain recedes, momentarily. She manages to heave herself into a sitting position. Where is she? How has she ended up here? That's right, it's a PE lesson. She has been playing badminton with Simone. She had Maths and Geography before break. She is in school. It is nearly lunch. She just needs to get up. That's all. Stand up. Put the weight on to her feet. Lisa has found herself coaching herself like this at the most difficult moments for a while now. For the last few months at least. She recites tiny, ordinary details like a litany. Reminding herself what day it is, where she is, who she is.

All the while blocking out the *other* reality that she is fighting.

Now Ms Plant is kneeling down beside her. The ruddy face, open pores and sagging chicken neck come into sharp focus too suddenly, inches in front of her eyes. The dangling whistle is right in her face. *How bloody embarrassing*. She hates causing a fuss; being the centre of attention is highly undesirable when you are thirteen.

'What's going on here, Lisa? What's happened? Are you hurt? Is everything alright?'

'Miss, I'm fi--.' Lisa's control over speech disintegrates and the sentence turns into a scream. She can't help herself, as the next wave of pain threatens to eat her up.

Jesus Christ, this can't be 'it', can it? Please no. Please no. Not here, not now, not in front of everyone.

And now the whole class has gathered round, like Lisa is the star attraction in a street performance, about to perform a dramatic stunt. And Plant is still peering right into her. Too close. It reminds Lisa of getting her eyes tested and having the optician eyeball to eyeball breathing into her face. She needs air, she needs space. She needs to be anywhere but here.

'Simone, run along to the medical room, will you? Get someone down here straight away.'

Simone is already on the move but Ms Plant is panicking, and uncharacteristically indecisive.

'No, come back Simone; on second thoughts, you go instead, Melody. Simone, you stay here so that you can tell me exactly what happened. Did she get hit by a racquet? Did she slip? How did she end up on the floor?'

Simone looks utterly bewildered, shakes her head, shrugs. She has no real answers. Why should she? Lisa hasn't confided in her.

'I just don't know, Miss. I was just about to serve. She was all fine one minute and then she just sort of... collapsed.'

Lisa knows it isn't fair on her friend to be questioned like this. She hasn't told Simone anything. Poor Simone has no idea at all. And Lisa wants to reply for herself, to answer Ms Plant's questions, she really does, but the breathing thing – it's all she can concentrate on. It's as though her body is attacking her from the inside.

And, oh God, suddenly there is water, and blood, pooling out of Lisa, and spreading into a vast ocean across that parquet floor. She doubles up again in pain and vomits into the streaks of liquid forming around her. The vomit smells faintly of alcohol, but vodka, as she has learned, leaves only the faintest of traces and is easily masked.

It must be clear, even to Ms Plant, with her limited gynaecological knowledge, what is happening now.

The baby comes quickly. The paramedics only just make it.

There is time only to evacuate the rest of the class into a nearby classroom when Ms Plant, having sussed what is going on so unexpectedly with one of her pupils, tries to regain some kind of control of the situation. Three decades in teaching have not prepared her for this kind of emergency. Twenty-nine other students in Lisa's class hear the howls – of pain, of shame, of horror – from along the hallway.

There are giggles and gossip in the corridors and changing rooms and surrounding classrooms. Phrases bandied about that are only half understood by the students that say them.

'Was that her waters breaking?'

'So disgusting.'

'She had a baby during PE!'

'Did you see the mess it made?'

'Who do you think the father is?'

'Dirty bitch!'

'I didn't even know she was pregnant, did you?'

'Do you think it's someone in Year 9?'

'She had started to look a bit fat…'

'Did *you* know about this, Simone? You're her mate. She must have told you, surely?'

'Lisa doesn't even have a boyfriend, does she?'

Lisa hears nothing of this, but she can guess. And so a child is born in the middle of that gymnasium, on a Wednesday afternoon, during a double Year 9 PE lesson, to a desperate teenage mother – an event heard by the rest of her class, and broadcast to the rest of the school in increasingly-embellished tales, as if the reality wasn't dramatic enough.

The baby is a girl. A tiny, little girl who weighs less than three pounds, and does not cry when she is born.

Lisa refuses to hold her, or even look at the *thing* that has come out of her. She shakes her head and turns away, stroking the parquet flooring instead. Now they want to take her to the hospital. They are worried about the baby. And her, of course. She's not interested in the baby, and certainly not interested in being its mother. She refuses to speak, refuses to actually acknowledge what has happened. Perhaps refuses, even now, to believe it.

She is in a state of shock. Both at the horror of giving birth in such a traumatic way, and the trauma of suppressing the reality of her pregnancy ever since she discovered it.

The ambulance takes Lisa and the baby away to hospital. A river of faces gawp through the classroom windows as the ambulance leaves the school site. They do nothing, just as they did nothing when Lisa lay labouring in the gym. Being watched in shock and horror and monstrous disbelief is something that will keep happening to her unfortunate child in the future. But for now, Lisa's classmates just delight in the drama of an interrupted lesson, a break from the routine.

For Lisa, so much more is broken – inside and out.

Chapter 2

At the hospital there is still no peace. Why can't they just leave her alone? There are bright lights, difficult questions and probing fingers. Once the male doctor has been and checked her over, a nurse comes and brings her a cup of sweet tea. Lisa makes a face and spits the sickly liquid back into the cup immediately. She hasn't drunk tea with sugar since she was little.

'Drink it,' insists the nurse, as though it is some kind of potion that will take away the horror. It won't. Nothing can.

The feeling of detachment doesn't lift. Things continue to go on around Lisa, though she wants it all to just stop. There are phone-calls, tears, utter disbelief.

Lisa's parents arrive.

They are concerned, of course, but also horrified and angry − and repulsed. Their daughter! She is only thirteen. A child herself.

'I told you we shouldn't have sent her to that school!'

It is typical of Lisa's mother to rake up an old argument to avoid dealing with the present one.

'I don't think it was the school who got her pregnant, do you?' Lisa father says, acidly.

'But why didn't you tell us?'

Because of comments like that, thinks Lisa. Because, because. She still isn't ready to face the real reason that she couldn't tell them.

'And how can we have been so utterly clueless?' Lisa's mother goes on. 'I'd have noticed if you didn't wear such hideous, baggy, shapeless sweatshirts all the time. I thought it was a fashion statement, not a way to hide a *baby*!'

'It just seems incredible that you could keep this from us!'

Not just you, Lisa thinks. As well as her parents, she has somehow managed to keep the pregnancy secret from Simone, from her friends, from her teachers – from everyone else around her.

Her mother paces around the white floor tiles and talks about Lisa in the third person, as though she isn't in the room. Lisa stops listening.

'But Clive, where did we go wrong with her? We gave her the best of everything. She is hard-working, high-achieving. A model student! She comes from a good home, from a stable family… she's only thirteen! She should have her whole life ahead of her. And now…' her mother tails off, because the premature baby lying downstairs in the intensive care unit suggests otherwise. It suggests carelessness and promiscuity and a very different sort of picture than the one that Lisa's mother has of her daughter.

Lisa hangs her head in shame. She hasn't thought about anything much beyond the birth, any kind of future. Her identity *is* bound up in being a good student. Her target grades for GCSEs are high and she has an exemplary school record to go alongside an excellent academic history. She knows this better than anyone. She doesn't need her mother to remind her of everything that has been lost. But her mother does remind her. Over and over again. She goes on and on.

She is a school prefect and plays clarinet in the school orchestra. 'School prefects don't get pregnant! Musicians don't get pregnant! She is not the kind of girl to get pregnant. It is almost funny how they are focusing on the getting pregnant. Because she isn't pregnant anymore.

The questioning goes on, but they still talk about her as though she isn't in the room. '*How* has she given birth to a baby while still a few months short of her fourteenth birthday? I don't believe this has happened. *How* can this have happened? How can she have done such a thing?'

'I didn't *do* anything,' says Lisa, all of a sudden, tuning back in as she hears the blame start.

She can't be blamed for this.

'*I* didn't do anything.' She repeats the statement, more quietly and shifting the emphasis. They are about the first words she has spoken voluntarily since that thing came out of her. And she realises how lame it sounds. But it is true – although she is still not ready to unburden herself from the secret she has harboured alone. It is a secret so painful that she hasn't even come close to explaining, even in her diary.

They are going to have to know, though. It is going to have to come out.

'I just couldn't tell you. I couldn't say the words out loud.'

Because really, how could she voice a truth that her mother would not be able to bear?

'What do you mean *you* didn't *do* anything. Babies don't make themselves. It takes two to tango!'

'Let Lisa talk, love,' her father interjects.

She has *had* to keep this hidden, she tells them, finally through heaving sobs. 'I had no choice!' Lisa pauses and shudders. 'He made me…'

But the admission is so much that she breaks down again and can't say anymore.

Her mother gets her phone out to call the police. 'Oh darling, it was *rape*? Why didn't you tell us! Rape is a crime. It must be reported…'

'Wait, love,' says Lisa's father. 'Let her finish what she's saying.' He senses now that the defilement of his daughter isn't the worst part of this nightmare saga.

But she has nothing more to say for the moment. Somehow Lisa falls asleep. It's both exhaustion and a defence mechanism. She is worn down by their questions and anger and tears and love, as well as the exhaustion of giving birth.

When she wakes up again, Lisa knows that it is finally time to speak the truth. She has run out of options. She doesn't want to tell them the next part, but her parents will have to be the ones to hear it. She has no one else to tell because Simone isn't able to visit her in the evening. In fact, she isn't able to visit her at all. Simone's parents have forbidden her from seeing Lisa, having heard a version of events that don't paint Lisa in a particularly good light. They don't want their own daughter tarnished by the scandal.

Lisa's parents themselves are already full of guilt at not noticing what was going on. They are more sympathetic now. They reassure her that it doesn't matter how it happened. They will support her. Lisa is not so sure. They haven't heard the worst yet.

Her terrible, shameful secret is that this child is 'Uncle Jason's.'

Through sobs, Lisa reveals every last hideous detail of the secret that has been so difficult to bear, that has ripped her apart emotionally, and then torn her apart physically, and will now tear her family apart entirely.

The father is Lisa's uncle, her own mother's brother, Jason. Uncle Jason. She manages to bring the hated name to her lips a second time. Uncle Jason who meted out his 'special cuddles' to his niece. She hadn't really known what was happening to her when she was raped by Jason, the weekend of her 13th birthday celebrations when all the family stayed in caravans down at Camber Sands. She is calmer now that she is finally telling the story. She can separate herself from being the centre as she tells it.

'He picked a moment when there was no one around to hear the shouts. I couldn't tell anyone because he's your *brother*!'

Lisa had no idea that she was pregnant until it was way too late to do anything about it. She didn't really understand the changes that were happening to her barely-ready body as she went through the middle stages of the pregnancy. She didn't even really suspect that she was in labour until moments before the baby arrived. She has been dealing with it all by pretending it is just not there.

But there is one last bit that she is still not able to say out loud. She has spent the last few months drinking heavily, in secret. She has drunk herself into oblivion over and over again. First in an attempt to abort the baby, and then in an effort to block out the misery.

She doesn't want this baby.

She can't look after this baby.

She wants nothing to do with this baby.

She will never be able to love this baby.

'We'll put the baby up for adoption immediately,' her mother decides. 'We can make this right. It will be as though it never happened.'

Although of course, it won't.

There are signatures, and more forms to be filled out. It is a practical thing that can be done amidst all the tears and disgust and shouting and blame. It is a way out of this shocking mess.

The nurse comes back in to take away the cup of sweet tea that has gone cold. She replaces it with a fresh one, checks Lisa's pulse, holding her soft dark skin against Lisa's pale, bony wrist while she does it.

Her mother barely registers the nurse's arrival. They must have a name on the forms. Would Lisa like to name the baby, if not hold her?

Lisa looks ahead of her. She really can't bring herself to care. She toys briefly with the idea of naming the baby 'Simone' but decides that would not be fair on her friend. The nurse's badge is right in her face as she collects the tea. It says 'Abimbola'. It looks like a nice collection of sounds together. It must come from far away (in fact, the nurse is Nigerian on a short-term NHS contract). It has an exotic resonance that feels miles from this London suburb and Lisa wants to be just anywhere else but here in her own reality.

Abimbola. Lisa has never seen that collection of vowels and consonants in that order together as a name before but there is a pleasing rhythm to it. And a nice circularity beginning and ending in that 'a' sound. It soothes Lisa to think about these things in an abstract way as words and letters, rather than to think about a baby as a living thing – or what her body has just been through.

Abimbola seems kindly. She pushes the second cup of tea towards Lisa a fraction. Determined, without being pushy. Lisa takes a sip. It tastes better this time. She allows the sweet liquid to trickle down her throat.

'A name,' her mother insists. 'We need a name for the form.'

Abimbola takes Lisa's temperature and makes a little clicking sound with her tongue when she registers a figure that is slightly higher than she would like. But she doesn't frown at her, or make a judgement, or look pityingly at her – as everyone else has.

A-bim-bo-la. Lisa distracts herself while they take her blood pressure for the umpteenth time. She says it aloud and at different speeds and breaks the word down into its component parts.

It sounds beautiful. And different.

Lisa feels only indifference, but perhaps if any good at all can come from this unholy mess that has been created then it needs a fresh start. 'It' being the baby. It needs an opportunity not to make the mistakes that Lisa herself has already made.

'Her name is Abimbola,' she declares. 'There. Abimbola. You asked for a name, and that's it.' She says it carelessly – as though she might have shown more interest in choosing pizza toppings. She ignores the raised eyebrows. She has suffered far worse recriminations today.

She falls asleep once more. Really, what more can they ask of her now?

But there is so much that Lisa doesn't understand. She doesn't consider the consequences of giving a little white girl about to be put up for adoption with such a distinctive,

African name. She still doesn't realise that she has permanently damaged her own liver in an attempt to drink away the shame and sorrow – and baby. She won't find that out until a little later. She doesn't understand that through the drinking and her decisions she has already damaged two lives – hers and Abimbola's.

Very quickly the adoption agency have a match. There are formalities to go through, but they are confident that they can cut through many of the bureaucratic processes. They have found a caring couple desperate for their own child but unable to have one.

Abimbola is officially taken away the very next day. She will need to remain in hospital for a while until she has put some more weight on and her respiratory system is more stable. She will remain in intensive care and then she can be cared for in the baby unit at the hospital until the necessary documents are in place.

Lisa doesn't say goodbye to her. She has refused to bond with this child – inside or outside of her. She doesn't hold the baby once. She doesn't even look at her. She never sees the almost translucent, glassy skin of her newborn. A baby so fragile she looks as if she might just break. She turns her face away when she hears that Abimbola has gone. She can be someone else's problem now.

A few miles away a young woman is delighted to get the call. It is a dream come true, the moment they have been waiting for. Yes, they can move fast to make the necessary preparations. The handover can take place as soon as the baby is healthy enough to leave the hospital. They can be ready to welcome her into their home almost immediately.

And that is where Abimbola's problems truly begin.

Also by Mirror Books

Not A Proper Child
Nicky Nicholls and Elizabeth Sheppard

Left as a newborn in a box outside Stoke City Football ground, Nicky's grandparents took her into their home, but instead of finding refuge - she was subjected to sexual abuse. In 1951, at the age of six, her estranged mother 'rescued' her. But Nicky's hopes of a safe and loving home were soon dashed, and her world became darker still...

As a result of her broken young life, Nicky spent years as a homeless alcoholic, ending up in prison, where she encountered Moors Murderer Myra Hindley and glimpsed pure evil.

Nicky's compelling life story captures her rare spirit of survival against the odds, and charts her rise from the horror of a deeply damaging childhood to a positive, creative and independent life.